MEN, WOMEN, AND COLLEGES

MEN, WOMEN, AND COLLEGES

BY

LeBARON RUSSELL BRIGGS

Essay Index Reprint Series

Originally Published by
HOUGHTON MIFFLIN COMPANY
BOSTON AND NEW YORK

BOOKS FOR LIBRARIES PRESS
FREEPORT, NEW YORK

INTERNATIONAL STANDARD BOOK NUMBER:
0-8369-2308-1

LIBRARY OF CONGRESS CATALOG CARD NUMBER:
73-167313

PRINTED IN THE UNITED STATES OF AMERICA
BY
NEW WORLD BOOK MANUFACTURING CO., INC.
HALLANDALE, FLORIDA 33009

**TO
MY WIFE**

PREFACE

THIS book, as the reader will soon discover, contains nothing new. Every address is several years old; every doctrine, much older. I am not bringing details up to date, because such parts of the book as deal with the transient are easy to recognize and hard to eradicate, whereas the doctrines are fundamental, and independent of time. Whether they are sound and still need to be promulgated, the reader will judge for himself.

L. B. R. BRIGGS

August 1, 1925

CONTENTS

MEN, WOMEN, AND COLLEGES

.•.

WHAT IS A LIBERAL

MEN, WOMEN, AND COLLEGES[1]

.·.

WHAT IS A LIBERAL?

ONLY those who have talked with the officers of the Harvard and Radcliffe Liberal Clubs can know how eagerly they have looked forward to this meeting. No club can be truly liberal while it remains provincial; and no club can be sure that it is not provincial unless it has some kind of free relation to a wider territory and a larger group than its own. For this and for yourselves we welcome you.

Here let me tell you what I regard as the hope of these Liberal Clubs — a hope which will often be threatened,

[1] Opening address in the Harvard Union at the first joint meeting of the College Liberal Clubs.

no doubt, but a hope on which much if
not most of your usefulness depends —
the hope that you will not forget what
liberal means. Though a radical may be
liberal, liberal does not mean radical.
Your prospectus proclaims wisely that
you do not represent any 'ism 'or 'isms '
— except, I suppose, liberalism. A
socialist may be liberal; a liberal club
will doubtless contain socialists: but
liberalism is not socialism. There are
bigoted capitalists and equally bigoted
socialists; bigoted Calvinists and equally
bigoted Unitarians. Only one belief is
essential to a liberal — belief in the
other man's right to his own belief. The
true liberal can usually understand
points of view not his own, and if he
cannot understand them, can at least
recognize them as sincerely possible.
When the Harvard Liberal Club held a
political meeting, it had a speaker from
each of four parties.

In a liberal club there is sure to be a

radical group; but liberal clubs make the mistake of their lives if they frighten out those honest conservatives who are eager, as even radicals should be, to keep their minds open. Driving off such people is not liberalism; it is illiberal provinciality. Even more illiberal provinciality is the contention that there are no honest conservatives. There may be tyranny in a monarchy, in a republic, in a board of capitalists, in a labor union. Anarchy, which would call itself liberal, may be the fiercest tyranny of all. In doing our own thinking, in coming to our own beliefs, we may think and believe with passionate intensity; we may try to convert all our intelligent fellow creatures: but so long as we admit their right to their own beliefs, we are liberal. When we cease to admit it, we are not. You cannot be even an intelligent radical if you go to nobody but radicals for your understanding of conservatism; any more than you can be an intelli-

gent conservative if you never talk to
an earnest radical. The present Colonel
Roosevelt declared the other day his
strong opposition to socialism, at the
same time condemning vigorously the
exclusion of socialists from the New
York legislature. Herein he showed
himself liberal. In welcoming you here
as liberals, we welcome you as fellow
explorers in the difficult quest of the
open mind.

An open mind in a still open field.
Able men, brilliant men, give themselves to the study of economics; but
who knows yet the true system of taxa-
tion, the just relation of capital to labor,
the just relative compensation of executive labor (than which there is probably no harder) and what is commonly
called labor, skilled or unskilled? Who
knows precisely where honorable efficiency slips into exploitation? Who
knows why no city or town is regarded
as prosperous unless it grows, though

growth too often means crowding and poverty and crime? Truth that is fundamental is still undiscovered. You ought to do your part in seeking it. The quest is noble; for its end is the welfare of mankind.

THE AMERICAN COLLEGE AND
THE AMERICAN UNIVERSITY

THE AMERICAN COLLEGE AND THE AMERICAN UNIVERSITY

In discussing the American College and the American University, I must say many things that may seem truisms. Yet as nothing is commoner than blindness to the obvious, it is well now and then to look hard at the institutions that are near us, to see whether they really are what we have assumed that they are, and to express what we see. 'Be the first to say what is self-evident,' says a sarcastic German, 'and you are immortal.'

Our conceptions of a college differ surprisingly. Once a man pushed by the line of students waiting at my office door, broke into the room, and said, 'Are you the gentleman that buys the soap for the University?' I told him that there was no such person. 'What!'

he exclaimed. 'Don't they use any soap?' To his mind a college was a huge boarding-school responsible for the toilet articles of all its pupils. Again, a youth came to my office with these words: 'I been working in Boston and I got hurt sos't I couldn't do no work, and so I thought I'd study for the ministry.' Without comment on the sacredness of his call to the ministry, I asked him what schooling he had had. 'I've studied arithmetic and geography,' said he, 'and I've studied with a dictionary some.' When I told him that he was far from prepared for Harvard College, he was sceptical. 'I'd like to see the books,' he said. 'If I was to see the books, I could tell better where they start off.' To him a college was an elementary school which might have reached page 25 and might have reached page 50 in the only textbook he knew. To some few a college is strictly an institution of *learning;* to some it is a purveyor of exciting sporting events; to some it is a place for social experience; to many it is, as I have said elsewhere, 'a sort of four years' breathing space wherein a youth may at once cultivate and disport himself until he is condemned for life to hard labor.' And so on indefinitely.

In trying to express what a college is and what a college should be, I shall speak first of the one men's college that I know from the inside, and hence the one men's college that I know. Harvard College was designed, I suppose, for ministers and Indians; but the latter, as James Russell Lowell observed, showed a stronger inclination to disfurnishing other people's heads than to furnishing their own. For one long period each class had a single tutor who taught it everything, and whose position reminds me of Dr. Holmes's famous witticism about the professorships that were not chairs but settees.

When I was a Freshman — a great while ago — the entire work of the Freshman year, and a part of the work of every other year, was prescribed, and the Freshman year was a good example of a solid old-school training. All of us had Greek and Latin and Mathematics about five times a week, carrying on two courses in each of these subjects. We had German, also, and Ethics, and Evidences of Christianity. To-day in the Harvard curriculum for the degree of A.B., not one subject is prescribed except English and two other modern languages. President Eliot, as some of us think, may have been carried too far by his own logic; but nothing is clearer than the infection of his ideas throughout the colleges of America, and the transitional position of these colleges to-day. You remember the immortal and graphic metaphor in the student's examination book: 'Dante stands with one foot on the Middle Ages while with

the other he salutes the rising sun of the
Renaissance' — a story so well known
that I should shrink from repeating it if
it did not correctly express the posture
of the American University.

The university in America is based on
the college, and is usually the same institution expanded. We have notable
exceptions in Johns Hopkins, which
from the first thought of the top as the
main thing, and Clark, which began with
the top and put in the bottom after-
ward. What should a university do, and
what part of its doings belongs to the
college? Some years ago, President
Roosevelt gave the Harvard Alumni his
idea of a university. The University,
he maintained, should graduate a few
productive scholars of the highest quality. 'Productive scholars, not annota-
tive scholars,' he took pains to add.
Scholars who shed new light, who blaze
new paths. On them, or on such as
promise to be they, a university should

lavish its resources. As for the rest, Mr. Roosevelt maintained, the university should do its best to make them physically, mentally, and morally trained men. 'What is the use,' I hear some one say, 'of citing Mr. Roosevelt to prove anything so evident, or even of saying it yourself?' Yet this commonplace of Mr. Roosevelt's is precisely what the universities, as I see them, are overlooking to-day. The university of to-day, carried away by its own development out of the college, has become dim-sighted toward two things: first, the relative importance of sound elementary training as compared with advanced scholarship; next, the impossibility of advanced scholarship without such training. Few men can be original scholars; many may, by long and highly specialized work, become learned, and may find little to do with their learning when they get it. Tempting mediocrity to the higher learning has much to answer for;

tempting it at the expense of the great body of young men who would profit by an education at college has much more. Can the university as a whole plead not guilty to the charge of such tempting? How many youths can it wisely initiate in research (unless research means merely competence in looking things up for oneself)? I would give a college education to every normal boy who has sense and training to appreciate it, and the means of getting it without dangerous hardship; I would give men of average ability who love study the opportunity to win the degree of A.M., especially if they are to be teachers; for the higher learning, and the degree that expresses it, the Ph.D., I would give every encouragement and every opportunity to the finest material, and discourage all the rest. Now, — and here I come to the second thing that universities tend to overlook, — you cannot make an advanced student of a man by giving him advanced work unless he is educated to undertake it; you cannot insure true graduate work by calling the worker a graduate a year or two earlier and shoving him into it half-trained. Mr. Roosevelt's chief function of a university is the college function; his ideal is the college ideal with extended opportunity for those whose talent, training, and character entitle them to the extension. The ideal of sound and strong manhood is big, simple, noble, practical. Some men realize it without college training; but college training is in men of the right sort an inspiration to it. It implies a large way of looking at things, a power of putting oneself into another's place, of taking for the moment a point of view not one's own, and disadvantageous to oneself. This power is — preëminently — the gift of a college which is cosmopolitan. Hence the untold value at Harvard and Yale of men from the

South and the West, from remote cities and even from remote countries. 'I've just sent a boy to Yale,' said an ex-Confederate officer to Major H. L. Higginson, 'after teaching him all in my power. I told him to go away, and not to return with any provincial notions. "Remember," I said, "there is no Kentucky, no Virginia, no Massachusetts, but one great country."'

The old college idea is something like this: 'Shake young men together; put them through similar intellectual discipline; lick them into shape; send them out presentable.' And this old college idea has produced excellent results.

Contact with other chosen youth at college may be quite as valuable as contact with professors. 'I protest to you, Gentlemen,' says Cardinal Newman, 'that if I had to choose between a so-called University, which dispensed with residence and tutorial superintendence, and gave its degrees to any person who passed an examination in a wide range of subjects, and a University which had no professors or examinations at all, but merely brought a number of young men together for three or four years, and then sent them away as the University of Oxford is said to have done some sixty years since, if I were asked which of these two methods was the better discipline of the intellect, — mind, I do not say which is *morally* the better, for it is plain that compulsory study must be a good and idleness an intolerable mischief, — but if I must determine which of the two courses was the more successful in training, moulding, enlarging the mind, which sent out men the more fitted for their secular duties, which produced better public men, men of the world, men whose names would descend to posterity, I have no hesitation in giving the preference to that University which did nothing, over that which exacted of its members an acquaintance with every science under the sun. . . . When a multitude of young men, keen, open-hearted, sympathetic, and observant, as young men are, come together and freely mix with each other, they are sure to learn one from another, even if there be no one to teach them; the conversation of all is a series of lectures to each, and they gain for themselves new ideas and views, fresh matter of thought, and distinct principles for judging and acting, day by day. . . . Let it be clearly understood, I repeat it, that I am not taking into account moral or religious considerations; I am but saying that that youthful community will constitute a whole, it will embody a specific idea, it will represent a doctrine, it will administer a code of conduct, and it will furnish principles of thought and action. It will give birth to a living teaching, which in course of time will take the shape of a self-perpetuating tradition, or a *genius loci*, as it is sometimes called, which haunts the home where it has been born, and which imbues and forms, more or less, and one by one, every individual who is successively brought under its shadow.'

What Cardinal Newman says of the *genius loci* hints at the power of academic tradition. Tradition does not necessarily imply antiquity. I know two schools for boys, Groton and Middlesex, which seemed to have traditions when they were born. I know one great university which seems to lack that element of romantic loyalty. An element of romantic loyalty it is, and an element of education too.

Again the true college life teaches independent thought except to men and women of false ideals and short-sighted ambition. It teaches public spirit, also, the responsibility of high opportunity. 'Enter to grow in wisdom; depart to serve better thy country and thy kind' is the motto on one of the gates to the

Harvard Yard. What is the so-called individualism of Harvard? Simply and solely the belief that development of the individual strengthens his power as a helper of men. To be anything in a good college, a man must do something for others than himself, something that his fellows believe to be service to the college as a whole. Hence, as has been said, one reason beside the obvious reason for the honor paid to the athlete. The athlete is, in a boy's mind, a public servant. The hero of the song 'For I am idle, beautiful, and good' has no standing unless it be as a Freshman — and he may never become a Sophomore. The mere student may be more unselfish than the football hero, whose motives are not inevitably fine, but he has not yet shown his public service except in quietly doing his appointed task — a service which boys do not recognize till they know what he does it for. The true spirit of Harvard College was shown some years ago by a candidate for the Freshman crew, who coached in studies his duller rival, kept him off probation and in the crew, and thus lost the coveted numerals for himself. Best of all it is shown by the whole life of the very man to whom the individual training of Harvard is chiefly due, by that great President who worked always for humanity first, for his country second, for his University next, never for himself — many of whose beliefs we may cordially reject, but whose life is the best expression we have of the true spirit of the educated man.

It is well to have a leisure class, that is, a class free to choose its own work, a leisure class that works. The idea that a college is a place of what Mr. Howells calls 'sterile elegance,' or a place of mere literary affectation, or a place of what the late Professor James Greenough called 'Britannia plate,' is no longer held by anybody who knows the American college; it is far more likely not to be a place of elegance at all — as the public manners of our baseball teams might indicate. Of course there are still persons who regard it as a place of idle dissipation. The truth is much nearer what a young graduate said to me the other day at a chance meeting: 'Some of us succeed, and some of us don't; but we're all trying.' Let me take my illustrations from the college that I know and love. President Eliot, beginning at seventy, when most men rest, to tackle the tremendous problem of organized labor, and telling the labor leaders to their faces their offences against the democracy and the humanity in whose names they fight; Henry Lee Higginson, a soldier like his friends Charles Russell Lowell and Robert Gould Shaw, once almost cut to pieces in fighting for his country, at seventy-five crowding every day of his life with generous words and deeds; Theodore Roosevelt,

a Porcellian man in college, a boxer, a
gunner, a soldier, a horseman, President
at forty-three, at fifty working his heart
out — with mistakes, it may be, now
and then, but with tremendous energy
and with splendid courage.

No college ever made a man great;
but many a college has helped a great
man, and added efficiency to small ones.
'On you, and such as you,' says Major
Higginson to the Harvard students,
'rests the burden of carrying on this
country in the best way. From the day
of John Harvard down to this hour, no
pains or expense have been spared by
teachers and by laymen to build up our
University (and pray remember that it
is our University — that it belongs to
us — to you and to me), and thus educate you; and for what end? For service
to your country and your fellowmen
in all sorts of ways — in all possible
callings. Everywhere we see the signs
of ferment, — questions social, moral,

mental, physical, economical. The pot is boiling hard, and you must tend it, or it will run over and scald the world. For us came the great questions of slavery and of national integrity, and they were not hard to answer. Your task is more difficult, and yet you must fulfil it. Do not hope that things will take care of themselves, or that the old state of affairs will come back. The world on all sides is moving ˙fast, and you have only to accept this fact, making the best of everything — helping, sympathizing, and so guiding and restraining others, who have less education perhaps than you. Do not hold off from them; but go straight on with them, side by side, learning from them and teaching them. It is our national theory and the theory of the day, and we have accepted it, and must live by it, until the whole world is wiser and better than now. You must in honor live by work, whether you need bread or not, and presently you will enjoy the labor. Remember that the idle and indifferent are the dangerous classes of the community.'

I am no blind worshipper of Milton; but I have yet to see a nobler plea than his for the active life of the educated man. Widen his meaning of the word *church*, and the plea is as strong to-day as two centuries and a half ago. 'But this I foresee,' said Milton, 'that should the church be brought under heavy oppression, and God have given me ability the while to reason against that man that should be the author of so foul a deed, or should she, by blessing from above on the industry and courage of faithful men, change this her distracted estate into better days, without the least furtherance or contribution of those few talents which God at that present had lent me; I foresee what stories I should hear within myself, all my life after, of discourage and reproach. Timorous and ungrateful, the church of God is now again at the foot of her insulting enemies, and thou bewailest. What matters it for thee or thy bewailing? When time was, thou couldst not find a syllable of all that thou hast read or studied to utter in her behalf. Yet ease and leisure was given thee for thy retired thoughts out of the sweat of other men. Thou hast the diligence, the parts, the language of a man if a vain object were to be adorned or beautified; but, when the cause of God and his church was to be pleaded, for which purpose that tongue was given thee which thou hast, God listened if he could hear thy voice among his zealous servants, but thou wert dumb as a beast.'

Whether the higher education pays, depends in part on what we mean by higher education. A Western father, showing some guests through his picture gallery, stopped in front of his son's

framed college diploma. 'That, gentlemen,' said he, 'is the costliest picture
I possess.' Few men who have such
a diploma would conceive themselves
without it or would measure its value
in money. For the great numbers, a
college education may or may not
pay commercially according as it is
strictly a *college* education or a college
education plus advanced work in such
graduate schools as do not definitely
prepare for some business or profession.
Let us look for a minute at the relative
cost of undergraduate and of graduate
education, not merely to the student
and his parents, but to the institution
at which he is trained; let us consider
the difference in equipment between a
college and a university.

A college, if small, needs first, a
moderate number of thoroughly human
professors, a chapel, a working library
of standard books, a few laboratories of
moderate cost, dormitories, recitation

and lecture-rooms, dining-rooms, a gymnasium, and a playground. If large, it needs also supplementary teaching, of which the Princeton preceptors furnish a good illustration.

A university, to be a place where a trained man may study any and every thing, needs all that a college needs, and much more: it needs professors of everything (human beings if possible), libraries of the widest range, all sorts of laboratories and engineering workshops with delicate and costly apparatus, a school of forestry with forests, a department of pedagogy, all sorts of museums, costly to build, costly to fill, costly to maintain; a publication office heavily subsidized to pay for printing what nobody will buy; divinity, law, medical, dental schools, perhaps a business school, and a great outlay for the maintenance of buildings. This last item has become so serious that, as people are land poor, so may universities be building poor. For some years, Harvard University has discouraged gifts of buildings without corresponding gifts for maintaining them. 'A man,' it is said, 'gives Harvard a building that costs a hundred thousand dollars; he appears to give the University a hundred thousand dollars, and in a way he does give it; yet, in another way, he takes from the University a hundred thousand dollars, since the interest of a hundred thousand dollars is needed to maintain the building.' Of course, this difficulty may occur in a small college. I knew one college which owned excellent buildings, and so little else that the President had to paint the floors, and the Faculty whistled for their pay. In highly developed, advanced teaching, however, buildings are more expensive in themselves, and more numerous in proportion to the students they accommodate. Larger outlays are needed for advanced students: it may

be in apparatus; it may be in costly
and exclusive teaching; it may be in
both. The additional cost of a university over a college in proportion to the
added income is little short of terrific.
This cost may be in part concealed by a
merging of the budgets for graduate and
undergraduate instruction (and no way
of keeping the accounts separate is
always possible); if definitely known, it
would, I think, shock many persons.
Let me say again at this point that I,
like Mr. Roosevelt, heartily believe in
generous outlay for advanced students
of truly high quality, and for no others;
further, I believe that not every institution should undertake to provide
for all such students.

Now as to paying, from the point of
view of the student. At a meeting of
Vassar alumnæ, an experienced teacher
of girls, discussing the scholarship system of the college, remarked, 'I do not
believe in taking a girl out of her

mother's kitchen where she is of some use, and giving her money to make a third-rate school-teacher of her.' In this sentiment I concur; but I also believe that for a healthy intelligent boy or girl of good character who can afford to go to college, it is nearly always a mistake to throw away the opportunity. It pays a girl, even if, perhaps all the more if, she is to be the mother of a family; it pays a boy if he is to work for his living. In all our great business enterprises, there is constant need of educated men; and though the self-made man with an enormous fortune is a familiar figure, it is not want of college education that has given him the fortune. I do not dwell on his regret, deeper and deeper the higher his business success, that his early training was not more liberal; I mean that for a better early training he would have constant use in his business. Some years ago a successful manufacturer of shoes appeared at the Harvard office to consider a course in Economics. 'I went to work at sixteen,' he said, 'and now I see that there is something in my business besides the practical, and that there is need of economic theory in it.' 'There are never men enough,' says a wealthy manufacturer to college graduates, 'for the best positions in business.' Another graduate has been urging college men to work for a great railway company; another devoted his speech at a Harvard dinner to dwelling on the need of graduates in the great steel factories; another descants on the opportunity for college men in the Mississippi Valley. Another wants the strongest of them in mining. Another tells me that he has decided from experience to take none but college men into his bank. An intelligent manager of a freight room declares that for a few months the boy he picks up in the street does better than the college graduate; that

such a boy has his wits better sharpened
for immediate use; that he is more
flexible, while the graduate seems slow
and unwieldy. In a few months, however, the graduate gets well under way,
and soon leaves the street boy far behind.

College education develops a man's
power among his fellows, his executive
capacity. Even the friendships of college life often lead indirectly to business
success through enlarged acquaintance
in divers parts of the country.

'The function of the college, then,'
says the late President Hyde, 'is not
mental training on the one hand nor
specialized knowledge on the other.
Incidentally,' he continues, 'it may do
these things at the beginning and at the
end of the course, as a completion of the
unfinished work of the school, and a
preparation for the future pursuits of
the university. The function of the college is liberal education: the opening of

the mind to the great departments of human interest; the opening of the heart to the great spiritual motives of unselfishness and social service; the opening of the will to opportunity for wise and righteous self-control. Having a different task from either school or university, it has developed a method and spirit, a life and leisure of its own. Judged by school standards it appears weak, indulgent, superficial; judged by university standards it appears vague, general, indefinite. Judged by its true standard as an agency of liberal education, judged by its function to make men and women who have wide interests, generous aims, and high ideals, it will vindicate itself as the most efficient, the most precise means yet devised to take well-trained boys and girls from the school and send them on either to the university or out into life with a breadth of intellectual view no subsequent specialization can ever take away;

a strength of moral purpose the forces of materialistic selfishness can never break down; a passion for social service neither popular superstition nor political corruption can deflect from its chosen path.'

Whether a *university* education pays is a different question. The professional schools are obviously needed for the professional men. The preliminary college training is, I believe, needed more and more for these very men as their professional work, by becoming more highly specialized, takes less range, and limits the sweep of their human — as distinguished from their mere professional — insight. Dr. William Sidney Thayer of Johns Hopkins University feels this so strongly that he advocates a classical education for physicians. 'Medicine,' he says, 'no longer resting upon a basis of philosophical speculation, stands upon the firmer foundation of the exact natural sciences. Almost

from the beginning the student of to-
day is taught methods, where a hundred years ago he was taught theories.
The enormous expansion of the field
which must be covered has led, naturally, not only to an ever-increasing
specialism, but to the fact that the
course of study which is regarded as
properly fitting the physician for practice is reaching backward farther and
farther into the earlier years of his
school training. . . . That when, in the
period of so-called secondary education,
it is proposed to *substitute* the study
of the natural sciences for a good training in the humanities, there is danger
of drying up some of the sources from
which this very scientific expansion has
sprung, seems to me by no means impossible.' . . . 'A familiarity with Greek
and Latin literature is an accomplishment which means much to the man
who would devote himself to any
branch of art or science or history. One

may search long among the truly great
names in medicine for one whose training has been devoid of this vital link
between the far-reaching radicles of the
past and what we are pleased to regard
as the flowering branches of to-day.'

Even an engineer is a greater engineer
if he does not begin engineering as a boy
to the exclusion of subjects which bear
no obvious relation to it, but which
by widening his view of the earth he
lives on and the people he lives with,
enable him the better to deal with
it and with them. Thus it is that a
scientific school in a university gives
something which an independent polytechnic school, even though better
equipped for professional training, cannot supply. The university background,
the association with the college, may
seem to distract a man from intensive
professional study, but it is an open
question whether they do not give more
than they take away. When the Massa-

chusetts Institute of Technology had a scarcely disputed claim to better technical instruction than any other institution in the state, it might still be a grave question whether the old Lawrence Scientific School of Harvard University, with great and manifest weaknesses, was not training men to a larger and higher success. I do not say that it was, and do not know that it was; I say merely that the university background, of value hard to estimate, was, in another sense also, inestimable.

A university, with university methods, is necessary for scholars; but of scholars in remote fields we must beware of encouraging too many. In a certain sense there cannot be too many. One of the ablest lawyers I know is almost or quite an authority on sagas, and is the better lawyer, if not for the sagas, for the quality that takes him to the sagas. What I mean is that we must beware of initiating into remote scholarship as the pursuit of a lifetime men whose scholarship is to be their only visible means of support. One pitiful instance comes to my mind as I write — a case of hopeless, shameless beggary in a scholar with no market for his wares and no spring in the arid desert of his erudition. 'All a man can do with my subject,' said a Semitic scholar, 'is to teach it over again; and if too many take it, some will starve.' Unhappily the higher learning has a strong attraction for dull people, — especially if they can be supported by scholarships while acquiring it, — and unless we take care we shall have on our hands what Germany was once said to have on hers — a great many more learned men than can support themselves by their learning. To the ministry, untold harm has been done by the encouragement of dull men; untold harm may be done to the weaker graduate schools. That I am not a solitary alarmist, there is evidence enough, not merely the testimony of some vigorous university teachers, but what might be called internal (and partly, if I may say it, external) evidence in the graduate students themselves. Do not misunderstand me. I have high respect for the degree of Ph.D.; I think the graduate students at my own university a fine group of men. Yet I wish we had more scholars of the older type who, as Professor James says, 'carried their weight of knowledge as easily as most men bear the burden of their ignorance.' 'You must be above your knowledge,' says Cardinal Newman, 'not under it, or it will oppress you, and the more you have of it, the greater will be the load.' I think that the scholar of the modern type has dangerously narrow resources unless a man of large capacity and at least some personal effectiveness. The scholar needs that rare combination of enthusiasm for his subject and recognition of its relative value in learning and in life. He may bend his whole energies to the discovery of the smallest particle of truth; but he must know that, though as truth it is to be respected, it is nevertheless a very small particle. Such a man will get his bearings anywhere. Oftener the scholar of to-day finds a difficulty which he may never overcome in adjusting his specialty to a reasonable scheme of human life in general and of a teacher's life in particular. For years he has cultivated a zest for research, for quiet, uninterrupted pursuit of the exact hour at which Chaucer started on his Italian journey. He has discovered the hour, or what is equally valuable, has demonstrated that some other discoverer's discovery of the hour is mistaken; he has secured his Ph.D., and looks down on mere bachelors and masters, 'scorning the base degrees by which he did ascend.' He is then rudely awakened by a class of lively Freshmen whose themes he must mark; or if there are not college positions enough to consume this year's crop of doctors and he is handed over to a school, he is even more inappropriate than in a college. Again, do not misunderstand me. The right Doctor of Philosophy, whether in school or in college, is the better for his degree and for every bit of his learning; the trouble is that the training for the degree frequently inculcates a state of mind, an attitude toward higher learning on the one hand and toward crude human youth on the other which, if persisted in, will be fatal to him who holds it. The university has begun to recognize the truth that graduate schools need to be humanized. Hence, the special graduate dormitory with its common room or general parlor. So often have young scholars engendered doubts about the human side of their work that the master of a big preparatory school, applying to a university for a teacher of Latin, was almost justified when he said, 'Mind! I don't want anybody that the Latin Department recommends.' He was afraid of getting some shopworn Doctor of Philosophy who might know no end of Latin and no beginning of wholesome human relations with the youth about him.

I have spoken of the high cost of university teaching, a high cost in which there is great waste. Professor Lowell, now President Lowell, used to say, 'A professor wishes to investigate the antennæ of the palæozoic cockroach, and very properly establishes a course of research for this purpose. In this investigation, as in any other, advanced students may learn his method. The next year he becomes interested in the stomach of the starfish, and very properly establishes a course of research in that subject. So far, so good; but he goes further — he still offers his old course of research in the antennæ of the

palæozoic cockroach. Nor is that all,'
says Professor Lowell. 'In time he
dies, and we send out to Indiana for a
specialist to carry on his admirable
work in the antennæ of the palæozoic
cockroach.' Now the cockroach is nothing, that is, nothing to speak of; the
starfish is nothing. The method is all. To
Professor Lowell's illustration one might
add that as soon as X University establishes research in the palæozoic cockroach, Y University (the Y has no
local significance) feels uneasy until
it has done likewise; Z follows, each
university supporting its independent
palæozoölogist, though a single university in a single year could royally accommodate all students who need to
investigate the cockroach's antennæ,
and every such person would be far
better off for the friction of other pa-
læozoölogical cockroach-loving minds
against his own.

It is easy to understand how tempta-

tion to become a university attacks a
college. Some local benefactor or some
wealthy graduate loves, we will say, Indo-
Iranian languages or Mining Geology.
He then endows his pet college with
money to establish there his pet study.
Expansion is always tempting, whether
scholarly expansion (like Indo-Iranian)
or practical, commercial expansion (like
Mining Geology). The gift may yield
about half a professor's salary; the college squeezes out the other half, pinch-
ing somewhere else. One advanced
study after another is added; ambition
to achieve something like completeness,
to fill out what will pass for a circle is
roused; and from that time on there is a
bitter struggle. Now it is right that a
college should give higher instruction
in subjects for which its geographical
position especially fits it. In Colorado
we might expect a strong department of
Mining; in Illinois, of Agriculture: but
if the ambition of every college —

wherever situated — is expansion to a university, we shall have a needless number of universities draining the country of money in unprofitable rivalry. Some years ago I was at the University of Ohio in the very centre of the state. It was growing magnificently. I never saw elsewhere such rapid expansion of a university 'plant.' It was costing the state much, and rightly. At the same time, two other institutions of learning were appealing to the legislature for state support.

The late Professor Pickering of the Harvard Observatory used to contrast the skill that men show in making money with the want of skill that they show in spending it. How many universities can a state easily support with public money? Should not a private citizen think twice before he founds a university, whether in his own name or not, within five or fifty miles of one already established? Local schools are necessary; local colleges are useful; local universities, though they may do good work, are nearly always a mistake. Outside the question of cost, it is infinitely better for the students that universities should be comparatively few; better even for the graduate students, who otherwise, when their salvation lies in study at a great intellectual centre, may be side-tracked into a provincial college with university ambitions rather than carried on to a resort for the ablest students from all parts of the country. No university can be at once great and local. Much of the value of a university is universality of constituency as well as of study. To fulfil its purpose, it must have variety in its students, variety of birth, early training, and early associations. In a subject that attracts thirty men a year, the men are far better off distributed among six universities than among thirty; the professors are far better off with five

students each than with one. (*But*
twenty-four professors will be out of a
job!) The money-saving in such centralization enables each university to be
secure. Suppose there were in the East
but half a dozen universities. (I dis-
creetly allow every man to make his
own list.) Are you sure that we need
more? Through such centralization the
university may be rendered strong; and
the college may be kept so. Nothing is
easier than turning a first-class college
into a third-class university; but not all
college officials appreciate the danger.
Among those who do we may count the
late President Hyde of Bowdoin College. As a college, Bowdoin can do and
does invaluable work; its function,
President Hyde maintained, is strictly
that of a college. If it became a university — it would be poor in pocket,
inferior in quality, and local. At present, it is a strong, healthy college that
knows its own usefulness, that keeps

for itself the American college ideal; that picks out the best of the young graduates and sends them to university centres for the higher learning, and, what is quite as important, for the wider intellectual association.

One of the sad things in our university ambitions is the attitude that they almost force a college to assume toward rich men. Every college looks for its multimillionaire, who may be noble and may not. Thus the college loses something of its moral fibre, of its independence, of its leadership, something of its sense of truth. Yet recognition of even the smallest particle of truth is the very basis of the university.

Thus I believe that there should be few universities, each drawing from many colleges. Moreover, I believe that there is no greater educational mistake to-day than that of our learned men in belittling the American college. Roughly speaking, the university teaches the subject; the college teaches the man. Of course, each teaches both. But the methods of approach to subject and to student are as different as learning and humanity.

Once more, when we look at our higher education, we note the growth of the university out of the college. The old American college or school of liberal arts which, with all its faults, has for generations been our best school of manners and of character, surrounds itself with costly graduate and professional schools, and becomes the new American university. The university idea as distinguished from the college idea got its impulse in part from Germany where many of our scholars were educated, in part from native love of scholarly research, in part from restless American enterprise, in part from the need of thoroughly equipped specialists, and in part from the longing of some college teachers to work with men who

love learning rather than with boys who
love football. As the building up of a
university absorbs the thought of president and faculty and the money of colleges, some men forget what the college
has done for our country, or remembering, believe that its time has almost
gone by; and universities vie with one
another in reducing the value of the degree of A.B. or in devising substitutes
for that degree.

Nor is it the university only that
threatens the college. The American
people insists on an education which is
visibly, almost tangibly, practical; and
the college must meet the people's demands. That an institution founded in
the name of Christ could ever have
divorced learning or anything else from
human life would seem incredible if we
did not know it to be true. The danger
of a college education may once have
been the danger of the monastery; now
it is the danger of the polytechnic shop.

We have then the college ideal dimmed by the university ideal; the college work crowded by the professional work; the college teacher inclined to set aside the college for something more advanced; the college studies changed to give the people what they want; the college income eking out the cost of the higher learning; and here and there a university almost ready to shed the college altogether.

No doubt the secondary school does more than it used to do, but it cannot be what the college has been to our American youth. Nor can the professional school of to-day vouchsafe to a student either college life in the American sense of the words or that basis of liberal education which, giving to the specialist a wide human outlook, makes him even in his specialty a wiser man.

The university must face the same problem that confronts the church. To be an active force in the modern world, it must deal with living issues; to deal with what a modern American calls living issues, it must not be over-theological or over-theoretical, and must show by its fruits that it helps men in problems of life no less than in problems of learning. The university, eager to increase its numbers and its influence, is in danger of being led by the people instead of leading them; and the danger, scarcely significant in schools of higher learning, becomes serious in the college, in that part of the university which aims to fit men for all kinds of good citizenship.

Yet if there is one thing for which a college stands, rather than a professional school, rather than a graduate school of higher learning, rather than anything but the church, and rather than the church except at her best, it is the leavening of an active life by a noble ideal. The college may and should teach, impartially, opposing theories;

but if it becomes a miscellaneous popular school, it abandons much of its strength.

I speak of no one university. I speak rather of a danger that threatens what I still hold to be the heart and soul of our universities, a danger to the very existence of such institutions as are still called colleges. The territory between mediæval asceticism and Yankee commercialism is so wide that we must be able to walk in it, avoiding the abyss on either side. We can keep an A.B., and an A.B. that is worth working for; we can keep about our college halls what Mr. Justice Holmes has called 'an aroma of high feeling, not to be found or lost in science or in Greek, not to be fixed, yet all pervading'; we must believe as eagerly as John Milton or Theodore Roosevelt that the educated man who fails to work for the common good is false to his trust; and year by year, as the plot of life grows thicker, we must keep in sight, looking deeper and higher with the eyes of our understanding, the vision without which there is no life. To show this vision is the highest duty of the American college. No school of law or of medicine, no school of learning for learning's sake, no school of theology wherein the word of God is too often bound, can equal the best college as an interpreter of universal human life. And so while we honor the university, let us cherish with her and in her the college, that part of the university which now stands most in need, the centre of all, the light of all, a lamp which it is for us to keep trimmed and burning.

THE LIFE AND THE EQUIPMENT
OF A TEACHER

THE LIFE AND THE EQUIPMENT OF A TEACHER

EMERSON observes that college presidents and deans are commonly men of inferior intellectual power. As one (or two) of these second-rate gentlemen, I am to talk about the life and the equipment of the class from which they are ordinarily taken, the great class of teachers. Are teachers, as a rule, mentally inferior? Can they be and be teachers? If they are, why are they? To what extent can they be the intellectual leaders of the world? There is obvious analogy between teaching and the ministry. The teacher should be an intellectual leader with a *sine qua non* of moral and spiritual vigor; the minister, a spiritual leader with a *sine qua non* of moral and intellectual vigor. The mere statement of these truths that nobody doubts reveals in a flash the chasm between the ideal and the reality. A few, like William James among teachers and Phillips Brooks among ministers, meet the demands of their calling; a few such as these are recognized leaders among thinking men. Many lead (or drive) the immature for a time, until the immature have outgrown them; then lead (or drive) the new immature, who in their turn outgrow and pass on. Creative intellect, even creative fire, is rarely their own. They are, as it were, the cooking-stoves through which the forces of nature are applied or misapplied for a time to crude compounds, which emerge from their keeping baked, half-baked, or raw, as the case may be, for consumption by the world. Prometheus nowadays is quite as often a poet or a novelist or a physician or even a man of business as a minister or a schoolmaster or a professor.

Lead us not into temptation. At the very outset teaching and the ministry, which by rights are high callings, have led us into temptation, and in somewhat similar ways. A poor young man with bookish interests and technically moral character, and without the vigorous courage to make his way, knows that in the theological seminary he may live for several years on scholarships; he knows also that without further training he can get a living as a teacher. Nobody in these days enters either profession for money; but some, I suspect, enter each for immediate support, and once in stay, partly through inertia, partly through unfitness for anything else, and partly through early marriage, which in their profession brings hardship and out of it would bring destitution.

The recognition of teaching as a profession to be learned like law or medicine through technical training, — even the comparative scarcity, in schools of pedagogy, of such artificial pecuniary aids as have at times turned weak men toward schools of theology, — has not yet rescued the profession of teaching by sending into it our strongest men. However demoralizing large scholarships for mediocrity may be, superiority is rarely tempted to run into debt for an education that will not enable it without many years of hard labor to pay back what it owes, that makes marriage imprudent, and the support of a family in reasonable comfort and in the refinement which superiority demands an achievement of economic genius. Beyond all this there exists, justly or unjustly, in the minds of intellectual men a certain distrust of pedagogy itself. Just as the minister should be the spiritual leader of his community and is often visibly inferior to half a dozen men not in the church at all, so the professors of education, who should comprehend all the forms of intellectual discipline, are not always among what an acute observer would call the best educated men in the Faculty. If the teacher ought to be a commanding man, the sceptics say, what of the master who not merely teaches the teacher how to teach but assigns relative values to divers and diverse branches of knowledge? How many men should we trust in so fundamental a question as the relative educational value of Chemistry and Latin, unless we knew that they agreed with ourselves? To the scholar the history of education is a sad but interesting study; the theory of it, a field of philosophical speculation; the practical assignment of educational values, a work beyond the power of the human mind; and the profession of such an assignment by a mind less comprehensive than Goethe's, a kind of impertinence. Meantime the professors of education may know even better than their critics how far short of perfection they fall, just as the professors of rhetoric, who also suffer from a suspicion of setting themselves up above their neighbors in matters wherein their neighbors are sensitive, and who are not always the best writers in the Faculty, may know beyond all other men their own deficiencies. In each case the professors themselves may feel as the late Dr. Horace Furness felt, that they have merely 'nibbled at the circumference' of their subject; but like him they see that nibbling at the circumference is all which any man may hope to do. If their deficiency is more patent than that of the archæologist, their subject at least is more human, and in its universal humanity, which exposes their weakness to the world, they find its stimulus and its charm.

This word 'humanity' brings me to the essential characteristic of a born teacher. Beyond all others the teacher who undertakes administrative work among students should be intensely human. This explains the close relation between administrative work and English Composition. Not that a teacher of English Composition is necessarily more human than other teachers, though no man is contented to teach this subject unless he cares more for the pupil than for it; but, even as athletic sport turns a searchlight on the character of a student, so does English Composition turn a searchlight on the humanity of a teacher. It is no accident that in the last twenty-five years five deans, or acting deans, or assistant deans of Harvard College have been teachers of English Composition and as such have revealed their interest in students as human beings. Enthusiasm for learning, a teacher should have, but this is primarily the interest of a scholar. Enthusiasm for learning may be catching; and so far as the scholar's enthusiasm is catching he is a teacher: but if he is a teacher in any large sense of the word his first interest is in his fellow men. To apply the words of Ben Jonson, 'It is not the passing through these learnings that hurts us, but the dwelling and sticking about them.' Of the professors of Mathematics in Harvard University it used to be said, 'The others teach the subject; Byerly teaches the man.' The others may have been superb teachers of mathematicians, may have extended the limits of mathematical knowledge; the one instinctive, predestined teacher was Byerly. When our University ship comes in (the voyage is a long pursuit — *Italiam fugientem*), comes in with its load alike of money and of wisdom, we shall not require of one man all the functions of scholar, oral teacher, and contributor in writing to the learning of the world. We shall have the scholar-professor, in whose laboratory or study the selected few may learn methods of research; and beside him — with or without the Doctor's degree his equal — we shall have the teacher whose life's enthusiasm it is to store the memory, to expand the mind, to soften the prejudices, to sharpen the insight and to strengthen the character of human beings, ambitious or not ambitious. 'A university,' says Mr. John J. Chapman, 'is a censer of sacred fire at which young men may light their torches and go out invigorated into the world.'

To be a priest of this sacred fire is a high ambition; but as Sordello learned long ago, there is

'No leaping o'er the petty to the prime.'

He who would be a teacher must love drudgery, seeing in it an inevitable and even an ennobling part of his divine commission. Without this understanding the life of many a teacher would be unbearable. People wonder why so few persons of high quality deliberately prepare themselves for teaching in the public schools. To me the number is surprisingly large and is explainable by nothing but an unselfish idealism. In our cynical moments it would seem that town and city governments do their best to drive out of the profession the upright, sensitive, devoted men and women who are its crying need. A young New England girl, the very flower of Puritanism, delicate, high-minded, and brave, teaches for a house-maid's wages. No man can serve two masters: but she is expected to serve at least three, the head of the school, the superintendent of schools, and the school committee. The head of the school may be distinctly her inferior in refinement, if not in knowledge; the superintendent may be bent on foolish educational novelties 'to make himself felt,' to show himself 'a live and progressive man'; the school committee may be ignorant, if not illiterate. More-

over, she has no sooner achieved a
scheme of life that accepts all these than
any or all of these are changed. The
incursions of parents and of politics, or
it may be of differences in religion, into
the school system have driven her old
masters out. Also she is forced to use
textbooks and methods against which
she inwardly rebels and is held responsible for failures of which she is
guiltless. If a relative of some one in
authority is so misguided as to want her
place, she may have to leave it; and if
when she leaves it she is past forty, she
is regarded as too old to be employed
elsewhere. In spite of all this we have
had many women of fine quality in our
public schools; and we have some such
women still: but as new opportunities
for women are opening on every side,
the more enterprising girls are going, in
larger and larger numbers, to other
fields as for many years the more enterprising men have done; and we are

more and more likely to find the place once sought by refinement and held in a high sense of duty usurped by mediocrity plus pedagogy. There is no doubt that to mediocrity pedagogy has proved a practical aid, and that the combination may do reputable work; but nothing can make up for that personal quality which is shrinking more and more from the shocks to sensibility and the discouragements to faithful service that our school system inflicts. In the private boarding-school the life, though free from some of the embarrassments I have named, is more confining; the salaries, including food and lodging, are probably a little better: but the requirements of dress and culture are more expensive; the marriage of the younger masters is as a rule discouraged; if they marry, the arrangements for their family life are inconvenient and meagre; and if their wives are displeasing to the wife of the head-master, they go. The

young college teacher after three graduate years in preparation for a Doctor's
degree is regarded as fortunate if at
thirty he is out of debt and can earn at a
good University twelve or fifteen hundred dollars a year by elementary
teaching for which his three years of
research have given him less equipment
than distaste. A physician or a lawyer
may begin nearly as late and earn at
first quite as little: but at fifty he may
be rich; and, whatever may be said of
the law, there is no denying that in
medicine and surgery lie such opportunities to help as may fire the enthusiasm of any man — opportunities more
tangible than those of minister or
teacher, along with a human intimacy
for which minister and teacher may
strive in vain. To the discerning physician men and women are known as to
no one else in the world.

Moreover, the college teacher of to-
day is expected to 'produce'; that is, to

publish books, and usually books that suggest the magic word 'research.' Research has its place; trained research is a highly educational process: but college governments should be grateful if they have some men who, rather than produce learned monographs which few read now and fewer will read by and by, strive first, last, and always to produce something in the lives and the thought of their pupils. In some colleges men already overworked are goaded into technical production, with a result, it may be, of either nervous breakdown or the intellectual dishonesty of scamped work. The greatest professional teacher the world has ever seen received no salary, conducted no research, and wrote no book; he extended the limits of human knowledge by transforming the minds and hearts of men; for he came that they might have life, and that they might have it more abundantly.

The picture of a teacher's lot which

I painted a minute ago is dark but true
— true, that is, as the mere husk of anything is true, true as the lamp that is not
lighted, the torch without the flame.
The secret of a teacher's calling is the
secret of any calling, the power of seeing
in it the light of the world, the transforming spirit. 'Colleges,' says Emerson, 'can only highly serve us when
they aim not to drill but to create, when
they gather from far every ray of vari-
ous genius to their hospitable halls and
by the concentrated fires, set the hearts
of their youth on flame.' Yes, and there
may be something to set the heart on
flame even in elementary drill. A few
years ago there died in Boston a teacher
named Bertha Carroll, 'to whom work
ill done was falsehood and work well
done was truth.'

As to the scholarship requisite for a
teacher, I confess that I am out of gear
with the times; that I am less attracted
by the new than by the old ideal of an

educated man. The new ideal is the specialist's; this no man denies. Just as among the physicians of a great city the general practitioner, the family doctor, no longer knows enough, and every stratum of the patient's body has its own protecting artist, so in a great university the balanced scholar of general culture is passing, and a group of provincial authorities, too often lopsided, is taking his place. We make German demands on a teacher's learning, without relieving him of American demands on his personal relation to the students. We seem at times striving for a chimerical hybrid who shall defy all the principles of pedagogical eugenics. Not that the new scholar has less time for human intercourse than the old; it is ever so much easier to be learned than to be cultivated, and infinitely easier to be learned than to be wise. The trouble is that the research attitude and the teaching attitude are in most men incompatible and that the modern scholar is trained to the overemphasis of some one point in learning rather than to the diffusion of sweetness and light. You can't (if you teach) be the first authority of the world in 'the antennæ of the palæozoic cockroach' without seeing those antennæ and that cockroach in everything and introducing them into a society beyond their equipment and deserts. In contradistinction to the scholar of this type, we may consider the late Horace Howard Furness, of whom I have just spoken. Even he may have been saved because he was not a professional teacher and was cut off by deafness from the thought of being one; but in hospitality of mind and heart, in the lavish giving of himself and his intellectual resources he was a teacher indeed.

As a scholar Dr. Furness sustained the delicate balance between minute accuracy and æsthetic appreciation.

'Culture in this year of Grace,' said he,
'is superficiality. The generally cultured man is a superficial man. And
why should we find anything appalling
therein? Can we not be superficial and
happy? Because we cannot distinguish
all the varieties of solidago — must we
forego the charm of recognizing Golden
Rod when it transforms an autumn
meadow into a field of the cloth of gold?
Because we cannot expound the theories
of the binary stars, are we to forbear to
name the constellations of the midnight
sky? Shall we close our Homer because
we cannot name the ships that went
to Troy? A little knowledge is not a
dangerous thing. If I cannot, for lack of
time, drink deep of the Pierian spring,
let me, in heaven's name, at least take
a sip. . . . Does Nature proffer us no
beauty in shallowness? Do the shores
of a lake sink at once to its greatest
depth? Is it not from the shallows that
water-lilies make glad the soul of man

when they bare their heart of gold to the rays of the morning sun?'

'Consider,' says Dr. Morris Jastrow, Jr., who cites the passage, 'that it was a man who had made himself the leading living authority in a special field who in his plea for a form of superficiality so difficult to attain that it is not to be distinguished from thoroughness, impresses it upon us that no specialist, however great, is therefore a cultured man. It is seldom, indeed, that they are not so, but they are cultured in addition to their specialty, not in consequence of it.'

Now and then a University refuses to bow to the new ideal, without sustaining the old one. 'I need for a professor,' said the representative of a Western college, 'a man who can rip up Keats and Shelley before a popular audience.' The true scholarly equipment of a college teacher is sound learning, human feeling, a missionary spirit (in the large sense of the words), and a culture that reveals itself, without pedantry, in every recitation, in almost every act or word. After all, it is a question of size in the man, a question whether he has first a touch of creative or, what is the same thing, transforming power, and next the will to discipline it — not to lose it but to bring it through discipline into its own.

'Books,' says Emerson, 'are the best of things, well used; abused, among the worst. . . . They are for nothing but to inspire. I had better never see a book, than to be warped by its attraction clean out of my own orbit, and made a satellite instead of a system. The one thing in the world, of value, is the active soul.'

.   .   .   .

'Whatever talents may be, if the man create not, the pure efflux of the Deity is not his; cinders and smoke there may be, but not flame.'

Again, 'Only so much do I know, as I have lived; instantly we know whose words are loaded with life and whose are not.'

He whose word as a teacher is loaded with life must have in him something of the poet.

It is hard to define scholarship, and impossible to define poetry; but each has a meaning commonly accepted though indistinct, which, for us who love both and possess none too much of either, will serve. We know pretty well what we mean by each word until we try to define it. A man achieves scholarship by thorough knowledge of books; poetry by imaginative power expressed in rhythm if not in metre. If we accept the old division of poets into the singer, ἀοιδός, and the maker, ποιητής, we shall see that on the whole the complexity of modern life is less favorable to the singer than to the maker; that, for the singer at least, the scholarly habit of mind is an impediment to spontaneity and therefore to poetry. The poet is oppressed by the feeling that nothing is first-hand. This rule has exceptions, but not so many as one might suppose. Mr. Kipling is at times inevitably a singer, but the question of scholarship sits lightly on his mind. Browning was at times inevitably a singer; but the scholarly habit grew in him stronger and stronger, till it often choked all his song and much of his poetry. Ben Jonson was at times a singer; oftener he was a giant workman piling Ossa upon Pelion in the vain effort to scale Olympus, which Shakspere took at a bound. These are illustrations only, not professing to be proofs.

Such things, however, are not what I have in mind to-day, though germane to it. I have in mind such matters as the relation of the study of poetry, the scholarly criticism of it in and out of colleges to poetry itself; for scholarship, admirable as it is, threatens poetry as theology once threatened religion, substituting stern intellectual requirements for the direct answer of heart to heart, measuring the unmeasurable, handling the intangible, materializing the spiritual. For the truth that the teacher loves and imparts is more than the accuracy of arithmetical fact. The man in Ruskin, 'to whom the primrose is very accurately the primrose because he does not love it,' cannot teach the truth about the primrose, since there is no complete truth about a living thing, or even about a thing we do not call living which does not recognize the poetry of it. Even the accurate man of science may miss the poetic truth of science. The late Professor Shaler, whom President Eliot called a 'fertile and adventurous thinker,' was as inaccurate as fertile and adventurous thinkers are apt to be; but with swift intuition he seized mighty truths. To him accuracy was not mathematical fact, but romance creating and filling the earth. Imagination warps facts, falsifies them, and transforms them thus falsified to exalted verities. The best mind unites minute accuracy with poetic truth. Dr. Furness had a mind of this sort. 'And that single word has cost you four months?' Mr. Owen Wister asked him. 'Almost five — with other things, of course, too. I have to be mighty careful ['Here,' says Mr. Wister, 'he threw into his face a delightful, comic expression of slyness'], mighty careful.'

A teacher should be in the old sense of the word a prophet, who reveals poetic truth, who opens the closed or half-closed windows of the mind. Let him feel his high calling, and he will never dally long with those doubts — those What-is-it-fors? — that in intervals (whether lucid or dark he scarcely knows) beset the possessor of highly specialized learning.

'In my more cynical moments,' says a young teacher, 'I think that the present-day attitude of the undergraduate is that of daring the instructor to teach him anything. He bets the amount of his tuition that the teacher cannot give him equal value in instruction.' You remember President Patton's remark about the attitude of undergraduates: 'You are the educator; I am the educatee; educate me if you can.' To transform the spirit that produces this attitude is the problem of the teacher. It requires patience, persistency, optimism, courage; it demands full acceptance of Browning's pet doctrine that romantic struggle for perfection is nobler than classic completeness, than perfection itself. It requires the power of seeing that no subject is too old to be new when presented to a new mind, and that the eternally fresh approach to a subject lends eternal freshness to the subject itself.

We all know that a teacher can hardly keep life sweet without a sense of humor — the best antiseptic for the mind and one of the best parts of that humanity without which a teacher ought not to be a teacher. Nowadays, with our musical comedies and our comic Sunday supplements, it has become clearer than ever that one man's fun is another man's horror; but even if a teacher's sense of humor is exclusively his own — 'a privacy of glorious light' — it is a choice and treasured possession without which, as the years go by, he could not do his work. If he can share it, as he shares his knowledge, with younger minds, so much the happier for all concerned.

The highest type of teacher should be a college president. A college president used to be first and foremost a minister; now he is too often first and foremost a business man. The minister was always a scholar; the business man rarely is or can be a scholar. The enormous financial cost of the higher education has emphasized too strongly the immediate money-getting power as essential to a college president. Mr. Eliot's report used to be called derisively The Beggar's Annual; and the mendicancy of universities has compelled their chief officers to beg from door to door. A certain applicant for a Harvard scholarship presented a testimonial from three fellow townsmen in Ohio which read in part as follows: 'He loves Washington as the father of his country, Lincoln as the savior of the Union . . . but his resources are short.' Such is the position of the American college, especially of the college which forgets that second-rate universities are already too many; that first-rate colleges are still too few; and that there is no wisdom and much poverty in turning the latter into the former.

A college president is supposed to

take an interest in athletics. When President Hadley's predecessor was elected at Yale, a New York newspaper remarked that a man named Dwight had been made President of Yale; that he was said to be a good man; but that he was 'wholly unknown in sporting circles.' As to the old ideal of a college president and the new, I may apply a figure of speech used by President Lowell for another purpose: 'You might as well compare a poem and a piece of pie.' Some think a college president must be a speaker, and, as a man once said to President Faunce, must 'go about dissimulating knowledge.'

What of a college president as a teacher, as a leader, as a maker of history? When a certain Harvard professor was invited to be a candidate for the presidency of another university, he consulted President Eliot. 'You know,' said President Eliot, 'that the name of a college president is writ in water.' The teacher checked his impulse to the obvious reply. One does not compliment President Eliot; but President Eliot, though too great to commend, is not too great to dispute with, and here he was wrong. The president who is a mere theologian is deservedly forgotten; so is he who is a mere money-getter. Dr. McCosh was a theologian; President Eliot, a money-getter: but how much beside was each! First and foremost, each was a leader. Instinct for leadership, with power to command, with wisdom, and with energy — all these a great college president must have. Yes, and one other quality often overlooked. President Eliot tells us that, just after his election (at the age of thirty-five), as he was walking down State Street in Boston an old gentleman whom he well knew threw a cane in front of him saying, 'Stop, Charles! What quality do you think you need most in your new position?' 'Energy,

I suppose,' he replied. 'No, you don't!' said the old gentleman; 'you need patience.' And after forty years President Eliot declared that the old gentleman spoke truth. One more quality a president must have — unselfishness. This greatest of college presidents never worked for himself, or even primarily for his college, but always for freedom and for man. Nor is his name writ in water; nor is President McCosh's. World-wide and lasting fame belongs to few; but of local and national fame these two men are assured, and, in a sense, of lasting fame. President Eliot's theories may be right or wrong, as Grover Cleveland's may have been; but in the history of American education President Eliot is as sure to be remembered as Grover Cleveland is in the history of national politics.

'Friends of the great, the high, the perilous years,' in one sense you will all be teachers, and some of you will teach by profession. To these latter I would say: 'You have received what this college can give in preparation for the life of a teacher; you have studied certain arts and sciences, and probably certain methods of imparting them; the technical equipment you have. Let us think to-day of the non-technical, of the spiritual, of that which links your lives to the lives of the world's greatest souls. So many teachers grasp the small things only, live in the back yard all the time, never see that the small thing, understood, is part of the large one and partakes of its nature; that even in the back yard there may be flowers; and that over it is the illimitable sky.'

How few are the great teachers! I can count on one hand all my teachers who had an inborn gift of teaching; one in the grammar school, two in the high school, two in the college. Not that the others failed. We boys learned much from them, and cared much for most of them.

Yet they had not the natural equipment without which no amount of learning or of pedagogy can make a teacher,— even as no instruction in versification can make a poet. The Normal School may give the profession a skilled workman, whose principles are sound and whose purpose is high. Such a workman justifies the school and does honor to it and to himself. From the school, also, the born teacher may derive that training without which his great qualities would lack balance. Thus, by rendering greatness sound the school may be justified still further; greatness itself is beyond all teaching. A well-known professor of English Composition complained that he had taught for twenty-five years without producing a single great writer. A less-known colleague replied: 'The trouble is that you are not God, and that nobody but God ever produced a great writer.' 'Great art,' says Ruskin, 'is precisely that which never was nor will be taught. It is preëminently and finally the expression of the spirits of great men.'

'It is, to the initiated, a self-evident fact,' says a contributor to the 'Atlantic Monthly,' 'that for the thoroughly successful teacher there can be but one standard; he must be an angel for temper, a demon for discipline, a chameleon for adaptation, a diplomatist for tact, an optimist for hope, and a hero for courage.' Professor Palmer in his essay, at once shrewd and beautiful, on 'The Ideal Teacher,' advises the constant practice of 'altruistic limberness,' a phrase which tells in little the teacher's greatest need. There can be no profession for which the requirements are more exacting. Consider the positively essential qualities in the master of a good boarding-school, and see whether there is one virtue that he can do without. If a man should expect to buy a single horse for the fox-hunt, for the plough, for the track, and for his wife's shopping, and should expect to buy it cheap, he would be about as reasonable as most of us are when we look for the master of a boarding-school. Our excuse is that, quite apart from the man's learning, the absence of any one virtue may be fatal. This person is in charge of our children. He must be kind, he must be firm, he must be interesting, he must be refined, he must be well-mannered, he must be courageous, he must be unselfish, and he must be so honest that nobody can suspect him of being anything else, so honest that honesty shines through him. This last qualification is rarest of all. Nothing is more depressing than the stupidity of disingenuousness, and the prevalence of that stupidity among well-meaning people, unless it be the notion that tact consists in saying pleasant things at the expense of truth. Tact is the union of sincerity with sensitive regard for others and is closely related to the Golden Rule. As a teacher you run constant risk of being misunderstood, since you must constantly keep dangerous secrets that are not your own. The only antidote to misunderstanding is the establishment of a perfect confidence in you that will suffer some things to go unexplained. Once let a boy (whether or no this is true of a girl I cannot say) — once let a boy feel that you are untruthful and, so far as he is concerned, you are lost. If he is an influential boy in the school, you are lost for the purposes of that school. However low a schoolboy's standard of honor for himself, his standard for his teacher is faultlessly high; and if the teacher attains it, and sustains it, and can give the benefit of the doubt yet not be blindly gullible, if a teacher shows his whole hand, or when he cannot show it, makes clear that if he honorably could he would, he may create among his pupils the conviction that to use him unfairly is not a schoolboy joke, but an intolerable meanness, a want of sportsmanship. He must be able to throw himself into the joys, the sorrows, the ambitions of the young — and the young of divers races, fortunes, and natural endowments. Yet he must maintain fixed principles, seen with perfect clearness, which admit infinite compassion without a moment of the sentimental or the flabby. In a line case between right and wrong he must decide, for his pupil and for himself, according to the very highest that is in him. 'It may be right,' said a college student, 'but it isn't stylish right'; and the phrase is worth remembering. The teacher's only standard of right is the standard of 'stylish right.'

Along with all this he must decide promptly. 'His great fault,' said a school trustee of a master, 'is indecision. Even a somewhat narrow man, who knows his own mind, gets on better.' Boys and girls like discipline, if they have confidence in its source. Some years ago Radcliffe College chose as its Dean a woman (now dead) named Mary Coes, who for more than twenty years had had the confidence of its students. She had thrown her whole life into theirs, never sparing herself, and what is equally important, never sparing them. She had frequently been obliged to communicate to them decisions, not her own, which they did not like, and which they may well have thought hers. On the evening of her election, half a dozen students in one of the dormitories were up late and learned the news. At a very early hour some of them marched through the dormitory with a guitar and a bag-pipe, routed the other girls out of bed (for nobody sleeps 'through' a bag-pipe), and had a procession. This roused the girls in the dormitory adjoining. Roses filled the house where the new Dean lived. Her appearance in every examination room meant a burst of applause. 'There was no mistaking the feeling,' said a sympathetic Harvard professor. 'The woman who can establish that relation with the students is the woman for the place.' He added, 'She's stiff as a ram-rod with the girls; but they know that she is just.' Mary Coes was kind with that kindness which respects a girl too much to accept from her a standard lower than the highest. The Dean of Radcliffe College did no teaching in the ordinary sense of the word; yet in the best sense she was constantly a teacher, and the relation that she established with the students is within the reach of any one whose character is as sound as hers.

To those who love difficulty the profession of a teacher is fascinating. He must be clever enough to keep the intellectual respect of the quick mind, and

patient enough to encourage the slow
one; he must not seek the self-development that people talk about so tire-
somely nowadays; he must never forget
that it is more blessed to give than to
receive — and behold, out of his giving
the self-development comes. It comes
in part from the mere act of giving, in
part from the obvious truth that, in
order to give, one must first acquire.

'The Son of man came not to be min-
istered unto, but to minister.' Of no
human profession is this truer than of
the teacher's. If he is a true teacher,
his earthly reward is the lifelong and
grateful regard of those whose eyes he
has opened to any part of learning or
of life. Willingness to be forgotten a
teacher must have, as Professor Palmer
says; yes, even certainty that most of
his teaching will be forgotten: but more
and more, as the years bring wisdom, his
pupils feel the worth of what he gave.
His learning may shrink in their eyes;

but his devotion, the exact training on which he insisted, his patience, even his absurdities, are recalled with tender affection. The tired, self-distrustful teacher thinks of what he has not done, not of what he has done; sees that he falls short in a thousand ways, and wonders whether he has not utterly failed. It is in this form that Satan must be put behind him. To struggle toward the highest, to work hard, and to love much, this is the teacher's life.

' Ah, but a man's reach should exceed his grasp,
Or what's a heaven for? '

After all, I am speaking to you mainly as human beings, rather than as teachers, because I wish in teaching, as in every other profession, to emphasize the human side. Again and again the head-master of a school, looking for a teacher of Latin or what-not, rejects an applicant for want of obvious human life. The true teacher is a man of comprehensive soul. Small and great alike are his, and small is an essential part of great. The God who

> 'plants his footsteps in the sea
> And rides upon the storm,'

is the God of whom it is written that without him not a sparrow falleth to the ground.

> 'All service ranks the same with God —
> With God, whose puppets, best and worst,
> Are we: there is no last nor first.'

'LEADING ONE'S OWN LIFE'

'LEADING ONE'S OWN LIFE'

'THE only thing we admire,' says Mr. John Jay Chapman in his brilliant essay on Emerson, 'The only thing we admire is personal liberty. Those who fought for it and those who enjoyed it are our heroes.'

'But,' he adds, 'the hero may enslave his race by bringing in a system of tyranny. The battle cry of freedom may become a dogma which crushes the soul; one good custom may corrupt the world. And so the inspiration of one age becomes the damnation of the next. This crystallizing of life into death has occurred so often that it may almost be regarded as one of the laws of progress.'

In our own day, set sharply against each other, are the leveling spirit of unionism and socialism, and the ultra-romantic determination to lead the full individual life with the unchecked use of every power. Sharply against each other, I have said; for though the former brings to the down and out an increase of opportunity, what it professes is equalization, which the latter pushes scornfully aside. Now just as surely as extreme classicism in literature begets a revolt to romantic liberty, just as surely as extreme romantic liberty begets a revolt toward classicism, so surely does either the degradation or the exaltation of the individual break in revolt from the one to the other, as now the multitude and now the individual raids the rights, real or assumed, of the individual or the multitude. It is indeed true that 'the inspiration of one age becomes the damnation of the next.'

The conflict is eternal. The very nation that drives men in masses to the cannon's mouth, the very nation whose 'lean locked ranks go roaring down to die' like slaughtered cattle as if a man

were of no more value than a ninepin,
cries out, 'I will lead my own life. Come
what may, I will have full experience,
full development of my national individuality. My impulse to unchecked
and expanding life is my right and my
glory; and it shall drive me on though I
lay waste the earth and strew the sea
with dead.'

It is scarcely necessary to say that
the position of a conquering nation is
supported by history and logic. From
the beginning strength of numbers or of
brains has conquered neighboring nations; and in our time neighboring nations are the world. Barbarous tribes
must be kept down or they destroy us.
Once convinced that we are the chosen
or the self-made pioneers of civilization,
we easily persuade ourselves that we are
the destined masters of the earth; that
the ultimate good of the earth demands
our mastery, to be achieved as other
masteries have been achieved since time

began, by cunning and by force. Inferior races are lower animals; and lower animals we kill for food and clothing or enslave for companionship and service. Some lower animals put us to shame by their higher qualities: but for all that, we are the superior race, whose advance means the progress of the world.

This doctrine is not Christian; it savors of the Old Testament rather than the New; of commanders like Joshua, who in the name of the Lord made a clean job of their hostile neighbors. But there has been no such thing as established Christianity between nations. We have been slowly feeling our way toward it; we have thought to see it near; and meanwhile this delusive, and alluring, and ennobling thought has been our weakness, exposing us to those who have relied on primitive instincts, hard logic, and modern science, and have despised the sentimental folly of an internationally fraternal heart.

I am not here to discuss history
and politics, whereof few educated men
know less; I am here to discuss the doctrine of self-development, the doctrine
of 'leading one's own life' as applied
to college men and women. I depend
on you to see the application of what I
have just said. If every nation insists
on living to the full whatever may become of its neighbors, the result is
either the crushing of all nations but one
or international anarchy. Whether with
nations or with individuals, this scheme
of life defeats itself; and he who 'leads
his own life' shall lead his character and
his happiness to their death.

Here let me remind you of the clash-
ing interests even in one man's or
woman's ideals. 'To be led by all the
ideals which are set before us,' says Dr.
Denman Ross, 'means that we are not
led at all; because we cannot move in
opposite directions, but only in one
direction. Consider, for example,' he

continues, 'the ideals of Equality, Fraternity, and Liberty as illustrated by so many interesting and impressive facts. Shall we be led by these ideals, or shall we be led by the contrary ideals of Superiority, of Exclusive Devotion, Self-Sacrifice? Shall we seek liberty of action, or shall we give up all thought of liberty for the sake . . . of some ideal by which we are possessed and controlled, some interest we want to follow, some particular work we want to do, some excellence and perfection we want to achieve, which is so important in our minds that Liberty seems as nothing in comparison, Fraternity an insistent and irritating interruption, and Equality quite contemptible in view of the superiority for which we are prepared to suffer everything.'

If the clash in one mind is so bewildering, what of the clash between one self-clashing mind and all the other self-clashing minds with which it comes daily in contact? For forty years I have been busy among college students; and in all that time I have found no doctrine more insidious than the doctrine that an individual must 'lead his own life,' nothing more plausible, nothing more fertile in prospect, more sterile in realization.

Like most such dangerous doctrines, it is partly true. We know what happened to the servant who hid his talent in a napkin. The young man or woman who throws away the opportunity of self-improvement and growth at college is a wicked and slothful servant: but the best servant did much more than make his five talents ten — he returned the ten to his Master.

One of the sad things in the theory of self-development as I see it in a college is its resemblance to those pests which, like war, destroy the strong. The athletic Freshman if infected says, 'A man [always a 'man'] must do something for

his class or his college *if he is to get on.*
I will go out for athletics.' The Freshman who has energy without athletic
promise says, with the same preface, 'I
will go out for a managership.' The
Freshman who has been led to think
that he can write says, again with the
same preface, 'I will go out for the college papers.' What he goes out for is
good; but he transposes end and means.
Instead of using his football or his poems
to help his college, he uses his college
as a means of advertising to his fellow
students his football or his poems, and
thus becoming what is called a 'promi-
nent man' in the class. Meantime he
slurs his studies. The reduction of this
spirit to something much lower than
absurdity may be seen in the undergraduate (not at Harvard) who, after
inspecting his sub-Freshman cousin's
attainments in football at a preparatory
school, reported to the family, 'He is
not good enough for college football; he
had better go in for Y.M.C.A.'

The studious youth, the natural student, may split on the same rock; for he may pursue learning quite as selfishly as his fellow student pursues athletics. Yet it is good to be an athlete; it is good to be a scholar; and in being either to forget almost everything else: the mistake is in forgetting personal responsibility, the one thing that should be remembered, and in remembering self, the thing that should, so far as is possible for us poor self-conscious mortals, be persistently forgotten. Moreover, in the noble irony of nature that very self-development for which we yearn is the ultimate reward of self-forgetful responsibility.

Yet we must not so far forget ourselves as to let the one talent remain one. However beautiful, for example, devotion to parents may be, it should not, except in a desperate case, tie a promising youth to the home town when the opportunities of business or of education call him far away.   There is a short-sighted self-forgetfulness not compatible with personal responsibility.

Much depends on the motive; and diagnosis of motives is skittish business. Of two things I am sure: first, that the doctrine of self-development for its own sake is a doctrine of evil, and, as I have said, defeats its own end; and second, that the self-developments of different individuals cross and destroy one another. Nothing is plainer than this: if everybody should try to have his own way, scarcely anybody would have it, and nobody would be happy.

'For pleasure being the sole good in the world,
    Any one's pleasure turns to some one's pain.'

Nothing is easier of logical reduction to the absurdity of chaos than the doctrine of full experience in life.   No one can have, no one should have, everything that his neighbor has.   To each of us much useful and agreeable experience

is barred, and we simply do without it.
Even the experience of a Shakspere is
in great part imaginative experience.

'As man is of the world, the heart of man
Is an epitome of God's great book
Of creatures,'

says an old poet. Yes. The full life of
Shakspere is the power of seeing and,
in imagination, of leading the lives of
others. Some portion of the power belongs to every one of us who misses no
opportunity of seeing wide and seeing
deep and seeing for something better
than the mere act of seeing. There is no
full life without human sympathy born,
it may be, not of tangible reality but of
the power to put oneself into another's
place.

Suppose you study for the degree of
Ph.D. and do it for your own development. 'Unto him that hath shall be
given.' The Doctor's degree is a big
thing for the man big enough to know
its meaning. It should deepen the

student's learning without narrowing his horizon. It should strengthen the basis of his opinions, training an instinct already fine, discriminating between the fleeting impression of a mood and the reasonable judgment that works undisturbed below or, if you will, above the region of moods, guided by principles of catholicity and truth. Just as the trained practical worker goes his daily round, revealing to nobody his bodily pain, his domestic anxieties, his financial distress, and almost forgetting them himself, so does the trained scholar suffer no transient ill of body or of mind to throw out of balance that power of accurate discrimination which the words 'trained scholar' imply. First as a corrective of the sloppy and the slushy, of indolent reliance on mood and on intermittent inspiration, the discipline of study for the Doctor's degree in a university of high standard is hard to beat. I once knew an exasperating undergraduate who would say, 'Last Wednesday I had concentration and managed to study a good deal' — as if concentration were a sudden chance gift of heaven without which a man is stark naught. I know a Doctor of Philosophy whose personal relations are disturbed by excitements that are almost brainstorms, but whose scholarship abides veracious, calm, unquestioned and unquestionable. Those who scoff at the Doctor's degree find their only justification in the Doctors who ought never to be Doctors — small men made smaller, first by the isolation of research, and next by the belief that, having become great scholars, they should not be required to teach Freshmen. These men should not be required to teach Freshmen — not because they know too much, but because they know too little of the right kind; because they are still 'leading their own lives,' whereas he who is fit to teach Freshmen is leading the lives of the young, the eager, the tempted, the hopeful, the disheartened, the intensely lovable and pitiable and enviable and human. 'He knows so much,' said Professor Kirsopp Lake of a learned pupil, 'He knows so much, and understands so little!'

The Doctor of Philosophy who justifies himself becomes, as he becomes a deeper scholar, a larger man. There may be, no doubt, a conflict between acquisition and humanity. Yet even if the Doctor is not to be a teacher, if he is primarily a discoverer, devoted as some investigators must be, to isolated research, he may automatically cease to be 'leading his own life'; for in the mere increase of knowledge he may become of high service to mankind; and now that the Doctor's degree is more and more the prerequisite to college teaching, the Doctor who is worthy of that calling must more than know — he must understand and love.

In our most imaginative moments we
may get glimpses of a world wherein
neither nation nor individual shall seek
self-development for self alone; wherein
no trade in fire-water or in opium shall
keep pace with Christianity in the coming of the white man; wherein nation
shall not lift its hand to nation except
in the grasp of friendship; neither shall
they learn war any more. In moments
less imaginative, yet so imaginative as
to transcend nearly all experience, we
can see an academic world so nobly
human that not a university or a college in it shall live for self alone, all
being members of one body for the en-
lightenment of mankind. About one
quarter of our intercollegiate rivalry
is healthy competition; about three
quarters is wasteful, belittling, almost
degrading selfishness. How much of our
intercollegiate athletic rivalry is such
as a generous sportsman may look at
unashamed? How much of it is the

spirit of gentlemen and of friends to whom we give or from whom we accept hospitality? The catcher crouches behind the untried, nervous batsman and reiterates, 'Weak hitter! Weak hitter!' The coach near third base puts his hand to his mouth as if to shut out the rude world, and informs the batsman with public show of privacy that the pitcher can't put the ball over the plate. The so-called 'audience' scrapes its feet on the bleachers and sings to its guests derisive songs. Such is sport among some of those who should be the best bred youth of America. And unless we are watchful we shall soon see and hear the girls do likewise; for the girls imitate the boys. A few years ago representatives of Yale and Princeton and Harvard met in New York as guests of the Yale Athletic Association, for free and intimate discussion of intercollegiate athletics. There was no attempt to make the number of delegates the same

for each college. There was no per-
ceptible difference in any one man's
attitude toward the students of his own
college and the students of another; all
talked as friends with a common interest, as older members responsible for
younger members of one great family.
This simple, natural meeting, in which
men's mutual relations were no better
than they should always be, was an in-
novation so notable as to mark a sort
of epoch in the athletic relations of the
three universities if not, absurd as it
sounds, in the athletic history of collegiate America; for here was a new and
refreshing recognition of mutual obliga-
tion and mutual trust, of the principle
that in athletics no college can 'lead its
own life' or forget that life is precious
to other colleges as well.

Should we apply the test of this
principle to the academic side of our
colleges and universities, how many
would bear it? Why should colleges

and universities be ambitious to teach every subject, however small the class in that subject and however great the cost? Because every university would 'lead its own life,' fully developed and richly experienced. Yet much of the richness may mean poverty and waste. I speak now not of that more elementary teaching which should be open to all competent students; I speak of those advanced subjects which require costly instruction, costly books, costly apparatus and elaborate outfit, an establishment for a few, who may be chosen but are not always choice. If on these few depended the advancement of knowledge in these subjects, the money might be well spent; but five hundred or fifty or five miles away is another outfit of the same sort for another few. In each case the few are so few that union with the other few would be not merely economy but stimulus and intellectual comradeship. Why should

not these advanced subjects be distributed among the universities with
some reference to local conditions? The
full life, with the college as with the individual, too often means the empty
pocket. It may mean also the lonely
teacher and the lonely student. Why
should the suggestion of coöperation
and distribution in advanced studies
seem millennial if not chimerical? It
is a simple enough suggestion based on
common sense and human sympathy.
Alas! we work for ignobler things than
these. Yet if we are Christians, or even
if we are not, we know what the founder
of Christianity would think of the
doctrine of self-development as it is
preached to-day. We know how far
from practising it He Himself was. And
whose self-development has approached
His? In the doctrine of this generation,
if carried to its logical conclusion, a
man's best faculties minister to his
moral and spiritual decay.

When I think of the larger academic life that we all should lead if we ourselves were large enough to lead it, I recall one man. Though he still lives — and works; for with him life and work are synonymous — I am free to say what I think of him, since I work under him no longer. You may agree or disagree with Charles William Eliot; it matters little. No man whom I have personally known has led a nobler life. It is, humanly speaking, a full life also, but not with the fulness that he or she who says 'I must lead my own life' has in mind. President Eliot has developed his unusual powers; always to the end of serving first, not himself, not even his university, but humanity. 'Enter to grow in wisdom,' says an inscription — written, I think, by him — on a gate to his College Yard, 'Enter to grow in wisdom [not knowledge merely]; depart to serve better thy country and thy kind.' The truth as he sees it he

speaks; the duty as he sees it he does.
By working not for himself, by living
not 'his own life,' he has come to his
own life, and more abundantly. In the
Middle Ages, as he once said, men
worked and fought for 'an idealized
person, a king or a lord'; whereas now
they work and fight for 'a personified
ideal': such an ideal is the college, the
nation, or in the motto of our University Cosmopolitan Club: 'Above all
nations, humanity.'

I have said 'man,' using the word in a
general sense; but what of woman as
woman? What of personal character
as developed in the higher education
of women? Rightly interpreted, our
colleges mean intellectual and moral
health, work, earnestness — constancy
of earnestness. Now, when the American college is challenged as never before, when the college for girls is accused
of making girls useless and atheistic, it
is well to consider whether we shall keep

down with the times, down to date, or shall fix our eyes on the ideals that fired our fathers' fathers and our mothers' mothers.

'Leading one's own life.' Ultramodern philosophy teaches it; ultramodern literature glorifies it; feminism reiterates it. Never was nonsense more corrupting than what is advanced under cover of that taking phrase.

Women, we are told, must 'lead their own lives.' To women as to men belong the rights and the triumphs of the individual mind, and the unconquerable soul. But 'leading one's own life,' as it is often understood, may mean in time everything that should shame woman or man — neglect of duty, selfishness, cruelty, disloyalty, infidelity. It is not self-development; it is self-destruction. On a large scale it has led to the worst war that ever devastated the world; on a small scale it wrecks homes, and friendship, and integrity, and love.

We have the spectacle of 'advanced thought' which leads logically to moral anarchy; and this 'advanced thought' is preached as the elevation of woman and the consequent uplifting of the world.

There is still room for him who said, 'Bear ye one another's burdens and so fulfil the law of Christ.' This generation has taught us the peril of progress without faith and love. Though a nation or a world shall shut its eyes to the 'law of Christ,' the law that 'Whosoever will save his life shall lose it' is vigilant and eternal. Let us give to our girls — as to our boys — every intellectual opportunity that the Twentieth Century affords; but let us not forget that some things in the First Century, though they may be discarded, can never be outgrown; and even as college-bred men and women let us not be afraid to proclaim that the one divine thing in the life of a woman as in the life of a man is human love.

ADDRESS TO THE FRESHMEN OF YALE COLLEGE, OCTOBER, 1917

ADDRESS TO THE FRESHMEN
OF YALE COLLEGE
OCTOBER, 1917[1]

No definition of education has super-
seded Milton's: 'I call ... a complete
and generous education that which fits
a man to perform justly, skilfully, and
magnanimously all the offices, both
private and public, of peace and war.'
Two generations questioned whether
he need have included war; this generation knows that he was right. Milton
lived three hundred years ago; and
nearly two thousand years ago a great
teacher came that we might 'have life'
and that we might 'have it more abundantly.' Put these two sayings together; keep them in memory; apply

[1] Delivered under the auspices of the Ralph Hill
Thomas Memorial Lectureship, which was en-
dowed by Joseph B. Thomas, Yale '03, the income
to be used for lectures to the Freshmen of Yale
College on the purposes of a college course.

them from year to year and from day to
day; and you will need no justification
for coming to college. They comprehend all that is worth knowing in college
or out of it; and they point to the reason
why being in — or having been in — is
better than keeping out.

It is an old story that, though want of
money may render a man unhappy, possession of it never makes him happy;
that no amount of money can express
the value of the best things. Want of
money may keep a boy from a college
education, though, if he is ambitious,
it rarely does; possession of money
never made up for the lack of a college
education. When some 'business king'
tells you that he has no use for college
graduates, you may suspect a lurking —
it may be, an unconscious — jealousy
toward those who have the one great
joy that he has missed; for, as a rule,
the better a man succeeds in business
the more bitterly he regrets the loss of

that which no business can supply; and the college graduate would almost as soon think of selling his children as of parting, for money, with his college life.

When the business king tells you that young graduates are conceited in their manner and slovenly in their work, he tells the truth about many of them; but even in commercial life they usually learn quickly, and soon rise higher than their less educated competitors. It is easy to bring evidence that the highest places in this country are open to college men; to remind you that our last three presidents are graduates respectively of Harvard, Yale, and Princeton; to recall the remark of the late Joseph Hodges Choate that he kept on his desk the catalogue of graduates of his college to keep fresh in American History. It is easy to point out college men at the head of great business houses, and to make clear that in business as in the professions college training is no draw-

back to success; but these are not the
subjects that I wish to treat: I shall
speak, rather, of college training as an
enrichment of life.

A wise woman talking of a student in
the college of which she was dean — a
girl not wholly to her liking — observed
that this girl had one capacity which
most of the others lacked: she enjoyed
her own mind. Young animals of every
kind (man included) enjoy their own
bodies and delight in the exercise of
them. In our eager American fashion of
turning recreation into labor we often
reduce athletic sport to an almost joy-
less grind quite remote from the un-
hampered expression of physical life:
the kind of thing that makes a dog race
round and round alone for very joy of
motion we rarely know after we are
twenty, for we have suppressed it into
staleness; and, for a similar reason, a
corresponding delight in the exercise of
the mind is retained by few.

Yet out of the grind we get discipline and even pleasure, of a certain sort. Free play of mind and body is set aside for hard work; and the enjoyment of hard work has become essential to successful living. From our athletic contests, from our lectures and examinations, we come jaded but trained, with less capacity for fun and more for the joy of effort and accomplishment. We turn play into work, but we like the work; and having learned to like it, we have won half the battle of life.

> 'The world is so full of a number of things
> I'm sure we should all be as happy as kings,'

says Stevenson in a nursery rhyme. 'Tell me where *all* the roads go to,' said a child driving in the woods. Both Stevenson and the child hint at a great truth. The alert mind responds to the fascination and the bewilderment of the unknown and can hardly leave one byway unexplored. The late William

Vaughn Moody, poet and playwright, looking over the pamphlet of elective courses at the end of his Freshman year, declared that if he should choose those studies only which were positively necessary, he might, by taking five a year, get through college in nineteen years. We must learn early that if we try to do everything, we shall do nothing well, and that the prison walls of the mind may be merely disciplinary limits beyond which, though we may not go, we may see with appreciative eyes. I once heard an undergraduate say with perfect gravity, 'Everything depends on the calculus.' One of the most eminent American scholars, Professor George Lyman Kittredge, pointing to a volume of the calculus as he walked through a library said, 'Don't you feel ashamed that you are going to your grave without even knowing what that is?' Clearly he was expressing his own ignorance, which he, one of the learned men of the world, regretted but could not remedy. For most of us, nothing that we have time to understand depends on the calculus, though we live in a more or less calculus-made world; nor has the student of the calculus time to understand the greater part of what to Professor Kittredge seems essential. Even in the subjects nearest our hearts, if those subjects are large, we must reject vastly more knowledge than we accept. Think, for example, how little is known to a great astronomer.

Sometimes when we see the humiliating smallness of what we can know in comparison with what we cannot, we grow impatient of whatever in our studies seems for the moment unnecessary and refuse to give our minds to it. Yet we are so made that we cannot get at the few memorable and essential and permanent things in any subject without learning many of the seemingly unessential and transient.

As in food for the body, so in food for
the mind, we need bulk, and cannot
thrive on highly concentrated nourish-
ment. Just as Nature lavishes and apparently wastes her material in producing a single animal or plant, so does
learning surround each significant fact
with a crowd of seemingly insignificant
ones without which the significant —
the abiding — fact cannot be compre-
hended. Some teachers are pedantic,
no doubt, and insist on trifles, or rather
fail to show that the trifles are so related to the essentials as to be trifles
in appearance only. On the other
hand, many students refuse to learn
the smaller facts that encircle and buoy
up the great ones, though they know
who breaks the half-mile record and
what his time is; they know Ty Cobb's
batting averages and the number of
bases he has stolen this year; they fill
their none too capacious minds with
knowledge of an ordinary sort, harm-

less — except as it crowds out better
knowledge — interesting in its own
way, but of transient value if of value at
all. Ruskin's simple and obvious question, 'Do you know, if you read this,
that you cannot read that?' may take
the form of, 'Do you know, if you learn
this, that you cannot learn that?' And
with it, we may ask another question,
'Do you know that *unless* you learn
this, you cannot learn that?' This last
question will steady you when in chemistry you must commit to memory the
properties of compounds that you have
never seen, or when in history you must
learn the dates of sovereigns who seem
born for nothing better than to afflict
the memory. Besides, the unexpected
value of what seemed a mere scrap of
unrelated knowledge, the sudden emer-
gence of apparently useless detail into
enlightening truth, is one of life's constant surprises. Some little thing that
you have not thought of for twenty

years pops up as the true explanation of some big thing in which you are working with heart and soul. 'All things,' says the Emperor Marcus Aurelius, 'are implicated with one another, and the bond is holy; and there is hardly any thing unconnected with any other thing.' Thus there is scarcely a fragment that may not be fitted into the mosaic of life (even Ty Cobb's batting average may come in somehow); what we seem to have forgotten we unexpectedly recall; what we actually have forgotten has left its impress on our minds. Shallow people talk as if their inability to read Latin and Greek five years after graduation proved that the study of those languages is worthless. 'Sir,' said Professor Kittredge to a man who complained that after ten years out of college he could remember no Vergil and could read no Latin and that therefore his collegiate Latin had done him no good — 'Sir, out of the roast beef which you eat each week how much at the end of ten years do you expect to find in your stomach *as roast beef?'* Most of us have lost our geometry and get on perfectly well without it; yet we are foolish if we deny its value in training our minds. Part of the student's problem is to recognize, and part of the teacher's is to help him recognize, the dignity of the transient and the small, not in themselves but in their relation to the abiding and the great. A narrow scholar may contract any subject to his own dimensions. Even an astronomer may deal with figures and with facts as facts and figures only: —

'When I heard the learn'd astronomer,
When the proofs, the figures, were ranged in
    columns before me,
When I was shown the charts and diagrams, to
    add, divide, and measure them,
When I sitting heard the astronomer where he
    lectured with much applause in the
    lecture-room,
How soon unaccountable I became tired and sick,

Till rising and gliding out I wander'd off by myself,
In the mystical moist night-air, and from time to
   time,
Look'd up in perfect silence at the stars.'

Though what I have said about learning is true, all men — good and bad —
have weary hours in which they say to
themselves, 'What does it come to?'
and a young man in college is lucky if
he is not beset by doubt as to the value
of what he tries to learn. No matter
how earnest or scholarly he is, he finds
in his college studies — even in those
that interest him most — much of which
he cannot see the bearing on his future,
unless he would spend his future in
teaching what he is learning now. Of
what consequence is the date of the
battle of Pharsalia, or even the battle of
Bennington? Of what consequence is
Chaucer's route in his Italian Journey,
or the name of Queen Anne's mother?
It is easy to prove the knowledge of

such details useless. Most of it evaporates after the examination; and what remains is not recognizably helpful. Many a learned thesis deals with questions of little moment to the world, for which world one answer is about as good as another; and the seesawing wherein Dr. X and Dr. Y come alternately to the front, each for the moment pushing back the other, strikes the ordinary mind as trivial and wasteful. When a certain carpenter, at work in the house of a great Yale scholar, learned that this scholar had, himself, stuffed the birds with which the house was adorned, he exclaimed, 'Well, he ain't wasted the *whole* of his time — has he?' Sometimes we feel as the carpenter felt. Are we Philistines for feeling so, or are we in a measure justified? The answer depends in part on what the scholar does, but more on the spirit in which he does it; in part on the discipline that he gets from his work as compared with what he would get from other work, but more on his success in relating what he does to the lives of other men, on his success in humanizing every scrap of his learning. 'All wisdom is the reward of a discipline, conscious or unconscious,' says Thoreau truly; but not all discipline yields wisdom; and there is no wisdom without human sympathy. The scholar may still be found of whom a modern writer has said, 'Patient and noiseless as an earthworm he accomplishes a similar inscrutable work.' The prevalence of such scholars in Germany and the unaccountable reverence for German scholarship at the end of the nineteenth century and the beginning of the twentieth, threatened our country with a large crop of such scholars, of whom some were ineptly detailed to teach Freshmen. The requirements for their scholarship are severe; yet of all scholarship theirs is the easiest to attain. Any persevering man with an average mind may be learned; comparatively few may be learned and cultivated; only the choicest minds and souls may be learned and cultivated and wise. The present war, whatever else it has done or failed to do, has broken the bubble of inflated German scholarship. Ceasing to idolize the Germans, we begin to understand that much of their learning is without form and void, and that darkness is upon the face of their deep; that they see without perspective and know without refinement and without wisdom.

Nevertheless even the discipline of useless learning is not useless discipline; and he who receives it becomes, after his kind, a trained man. When American boys began their Latin in learning Andrews and Stoddard's Latin grammar by heart — rules, exceptions, and all — they were taught by a method that we abhor. Yet such of them as succeeded in the prodigious task could thereafter grapple with anything that required memory alone; and memory is not so despicably unworthy of cultivation as some lazy people — and some modern educators — would have it. All serious work of mind or body yields training. The uninspired scholar, the 'grind' pure and simple, wastes his time in so far as he shuts his eyes to the human and divine significance of his work, a significance which might leaven every bit of it; that is, he might get more out of his time than he does, — or rather somebody else might get more out of it. But for youths who frequent musical comedies and dawdle over colored supplements to allege that he wastes his time is downright effrontery. Now and then a scholar does his minute work with a kind of exaltation, even though the significance that he sees in it is more or less unreal. If you read Browning's 'A Grammarian's Funeral,' you will see what I mean. It is the story of a famous scholar in the revival of learning known as the Renaissance; of a fanatical grind, to whom Greek particles were meat and drink and religion, for their own sake rather than for their meaning to men and women.

I have assumed that a student studies; and I make no apology for the assumption. Let me add that it furthers efficiency in study, and in life generally, to work with a time-table. Allow so much time for each subject, know just when you are to study it, feel limited, and you accomplish more. Certainly you waste less time in transitions. Also, when you have held to your time-table, what remains of the day is your very own — or the football captain's, if you choose — yours to dispose of as you think best, and you have earned it. Get into the habit of crashing right through all hindrances and doing your day's work. Once more let me quote the proud advertisement of the old steam-

boat line: 'In summer or winter, in
storm or calm, the Commonwealth and
the Plymouth Rock invariably make
the passage.' This is merely bringing
into the routine of study that quality
which in athletics makes a man a hero
— gameness.

Much of this time that is your own
you may and should give to friendship;
and as the years go by you will discover
that it is not the friends you loaf with,
but the friends you work with who
mean most to you. By and by it may be
the friends you work with, whom you
choose to loaf with, if you loaf at all.
Just so it is not necessarily the girl with
whom you dance most happily, but
rather the girl with whom you work
most happily whom you are likely to be
happy in marrying; and much of the
trouble between husbands and wives is
the natural result of dancing friendships, agreeable but superficial, rather
than working friendships which bring a
high test of companionship.

The question of friends raises the question of fraternities and clubs. Knowing little of clubs from the inside — and nothing of fraternities — and not being naturally a club man, I have no right to say much on the subject. To some men 'Bones,' for example, is holy ground; and as they seem intelligent men, they doubtless have some excuse for their reverence. What I have a right to say is general — namely, that no club can ever exist which it pays to get into through sacrifice of personal independence and self-respect. Do something worth doing, do it as well as you can, and let the club question take care of itself. If a club wants you and you think that you shall be happier for joining it, join it by all means, remembering that you cannot honorably be happier for joining it unless you can afford the money. If it does not want you, you, if you are a man, do not want it. Live among those — the best of those — who wish for your society, not among those who tolerate it. Go about your business, remembering that a university offers many consolation prizes and that time rectifies much. Some Harvard men who as undergraduates could not have got into the Hasty Pudding Club for love or money are men with whom to-day it is an honor for their classmates in the club to associate. Sometimes recognition comes before you graduate; and, in the words of a man who entered Harvard almost unknown and received the best of all class offices, 'You may have to dodge the honors instead of working for them.'

The forming of friendships is for many of us a delicate and embarrassing matter. Some men form them through a natural gift, which seems to come as easily as speech; but most of us, in the presence of those whom we should like to please, are self-conscious and shy. 'Shy!' said President Lowell to the

Harvard Freshmen. 'Of course you're shy! The queer thing about a Freshman is that he thinks he's the only one that's shy.' Mr. Chesterton tells us that a very young man usually regards himself as a Robinson Crusoe; that is, I suppose, as somebody whose experience is quite different from anybody's else or, if you please, as somebody who lives on an island by himself — insulated, isolated, in the original sense of those words. So far as we can judge, nobody's experience is precisely duplicated. 'X bears pain better than Y,' we say, not knowing whether X ever had Y's pain. Yet as we grow older we discover that many griefs and pains which we have regarded as specialties of our own (and may even have nursed and petted as such) are as nearly universal as the morning newspaper. We get our own copies; that is all. Only a very few of us escape the embarrassment of shyness: and those who put on the boldest front may be inwardly the most self-distrustful; bravado, until detected, is an admirable cover for embarrassment. A sensitive youth tortures himself about some real or fancied social blunder, some greenness, some harmless absurdity fit to laugh at and quite unworthy of remorse — which we should keep for our sins. Thackeray has helped some of us by pointing out that diffidence is a form of self-conceit; that we should not be bashful if we were not thinking too much about ourselves. It is he who observes that we never thoroughly enjoy the society of women until we are old enough not to be ill at ease as to the impression which we are making on them. These observations contain wholesome truth; yet I for one had rather see a youth a little shy than afflicted with 'callow knowingness.' A perfectly self-assured Freshman is over-ripe while he is still green, and makes offensive blunders while he should be making lovable ones. As a man who has suffered all his life from being scared too much, I maintain that being scared a little is stimulating and wholesome, especially in the young. 'I wonder,' said a young teacher, 'whether the time will ever come when my knees don't shake under me as I go to meet my classes.' 'If that time comes, young man,' said the old friend to whom he spoke, 'quit meeting your classes.' The late Phillips Brooks, probably the greatest preacher of his day, was perfect master of himself and his audience as soon as he had stepped to platform or to pulpit; but before that time he suffered misery. One of the most brilliant teachers in America gave not long ago a Commencement address which was received with unbounded enthusiasm. It was avowedly an address of only fifteen minutes; but for two days he had been utterly wretched about it, declaring that it was 'all cackle and no egg.' I have

known only one or two after-dinner
speakers who admitted that they thoroughly liked to speak. Most speakers
await their turns dismally, little relishing their food and relishing still less the
conversation of their neighbors to whom
they are trying to be polite while rally-
ing the confused and routed inmates of
their minds in the effort to be ready
for the call. Yet their suffering, which
amounts in some cases to agony, does
no harm to their speeches. Their standard being far beyond their attainment,
they anxiously and constantly try to
improve, whereas the perfectly fluent
and self-possessed man tends not to
improve but to deteriorate or even to
decay. He can always, as the saying is,
'get by.' Not having to work, he does
not work; and he grows wordier and
wordier, and emptier and emptier as
time goes on. Don't be afraid of being afraid; it is not half such a draw-
back as you think, nor have you a mo-

nopoly of it. It tends to put people into sympathy with you; it is a good thing to fight with and keep down, not a good thing to be without altogether, for without a touch of it you can't understand humankind. A sensitive nervous organization, if you don't pamper it but command it, will help you do the best work that you ever do, better work than can ever be done by men that have not this difficult servant who when used indiscreetly is always ready for strikes and lock-outs and anarchy and when used wisely renders the finest service in the world.

The bearing of all this on friendship is not so remote as it seems. Just as a youth in love musters courage for what, before he was in love, would have struck him as rank and impossible audacity, so a youth who wishes to make friends with another youth must not yield to fear, and through shyness beat a retreat; yet if in his advances he shows a little of the hesitation that he feels, he will do no harm. At least let him remember that the other youth is embarrassed also, as many an athlete has plucked up heart at the sudden thought that his adversary is as scared as he. Let him remember also that a perfect understanding takes time. When we arrive at that stage of friendship which requires no talking for talking's sake, we are friends indeed.

As an older man who has seen many young men in their chastening hours I give you one piece of advice with which you are already familiar: keep in training — moderate, reasonable training — all the time. Many of you, no doubt, think that I say this professionally, like the minister who accepts as his business the job of telling men to be good: but the minister who is worth his salt does not tell men to be good because it is his business; he makes it his business because he believes in it. What

I say now is based on common sense, not necessarily on morals except in so far as common sense and morals are one and the same. 'I don't care about the morality of it, Tom,' said a distinguished surgeon to an athlete who was going wrong. 'I don't care about the morality of it; but it doesn't pay.' Now I do care, and I hope that you care, about the morality of it. I do care whether you do or do not betray the trust of those who send you hither, whether you are or are not to be fit husbands to your wives, fit fathers to your children. I do care about the morality of it, *and* it doesn't pay. It doesn't pay — except in sleep — not to know what you are doing, for you may be doing what to you and to others will bring lifelong regret; it doesn't pay to put an enemy in your mouth to steal away your brains; it doesn't pay physically, mentally, morally, — and certainly it doesn't pay financially, — to

run with dubious women or worse, to
sup with chorus girls after the theatre;
it doesn't pay to be victimized, or to put
yourself into a position in which not to
be victimized becomes a matter of luck;
it doesn't pay to keep dreadfully late
hours and be a nervous wreck before
your time; it doesn't pay to need all
sorts of artificial excitement as a stimu-
lant to life when at your age life itself
should be full of zest — precisely as it
doesn't pay to lose appetite for meat
and bread and vegetables unless they
are covered with hot sauces or India
relish — and it doesn't pay, while you
are young, to get into such nervous
condition that you cannot use your
minds until sensible people are in bed.
Many estimable men have once or twice
been drunk; many admirable scholars
turn night into day and day into night:
yet the general rule holds good. 'I object to getting up early as part of a
definition of virtue,' a friend of mine

remarked. Nevertheless there is much to be said for a day that begins early and ends not late, or why should military and athletic trainers insist on it? The modern society ball to which young people go at midnight and from which they emerge at five or six A.M., after limitless champagne in side-rooms at three, is something for which society, and especially society's matrons, may well be called to account. A society girl may lie in bed all the next day and sleep it off; a man — the college student who goes to such balls — has much else to do. He has his classes, which he cannot cut with safety, and his work, for which he finds neither heart nor head. Besides, if he keeps up the kind of life that I have indicated, he gets so stale that he can do nothing without stimulus, for his mind loses all elasticity. In such condition a man lacks power of discrimination. Questions of right and wrong he blurs; for morally and mentally he grows nearsighted. Half the wrong things we do, half the 'fool' things we do, are the direct result of the muddle we get into when we have abused our nerves and have thus incapacitated them. It is a 'fool thing' to put yourself in the way of doing a 'fool thing.' The moment that you lose the power to discriminate you make any and every kind of 'break.' What all people used to call, and some still call, the devil, is too alert to let such a moment go by; for the devil, whatever his failings, never fails to know and to seize his opportunities.

This explains the need of vacations. 'I can do my year's work in eleven months,' said a famous lawyer; 'I can't do it in twelve.' This, wholly outside of religious restrictions, is why Sunday is valuable as a day of refreshment whether in church or in the woods, and why the week-end plays so important a part in modern life. With characteristic want of sense as to what relieves the mind, we turn Sundays and week-ends into exhausting work, much as we treat the recreative sport of baseball and football; but even the work, so long as it differs from our other work, brings some relief, though not enough.

College students rarely need prodding as to the value of vacations; they present all sorts of reasons for lengthening every holiday at both ends and celebrating through half a week the single day devoted to the memory of Washington. Oculists, dentists (the only dentists skilful enough for them to patronize) can spare no time for them except a day or two just before or just after the regular holidays; sisters' weddings in distant cities are neatly placed a day or two before or after the spring recess, not to mention ushers' dinners, of which the less said the better. Yet college students, though they like to get off, do not appreciate judicious periods of rest. At about one A.M. the undergraduate has 'all the time there is.' 'The worst trouble with our students,' said a professor who was wiser than he seemed, 'is want of sleep.' Much of what is called laziness in students is the protest of neglected Nature. I remember saying to myself as a child that when I was grown up I would never go to bed till twelve o'clock; and many a college year of unremitting work has brought its retribution.

My point is that neglected Nature takes her revenge in warping judgment, weakening will, undermining common sense, and dislocating the distinction between right and wrong. 'He did it under pressure,' people say. Yes, he always does. What we particularly wish we had not done, we have done under pressure; and the worst part of the pressure is that humiliating stupidity which renders us, in all ways, inefficient. Everybody knows that when he reaches a certain point of weariness, he mislays things, cannot find what is in plain sight, and cannot get on with either his work or his play or his neighbors. Among the things that he mislays is his mind; and without mind there is no strength of character.

In these times to talk of athletics may seem trivial. A young graduate told me the other day that a Yale-Harvard football game now would seem like fiddling while Rome is burning. Yet athletics have played and will play a great part in college life; and to athletics we owe much of our manhood. Even to you, the youngest students, military training comes first just now, when relative values are suddenly transposed; yet so far as military training permits, students will do well to cultivate athletics — no longer as a task but as a relief. Home games in which you win if you can but don't suffer if you can't, intercollegiate games of the same informal character, are worth trying now. This war makes molehills of many things that posed as mountains; and our stupendous Yale and Princeton and Harvard games seem not so stupendous after all. In one way they are important still: the heroes of the gridiron are among the first to answer the call of the trumpet, and who shall say that the training and the intensity of the old contest have been in vain? Yet even those of us who loved the old contest and gloried in much that it brought forth have known that it filled too large a place in the minds of our students and far too large a place in the minds of the public, which should have little concern with it. We can cut down luxuries, limit the cost of coaching, spend liberally and not wastefully. Also, we can remember that Yale men and Princeton men and Harvard men, even as they stand together for life or death to defend the liberty of the world, must stand together as students and as sportsmen. Stirred by a great cause, they spring forward as one man; they march, they fight, they stake their all, as brothers in arms. How could they ever haggle over dates and umpires and eligibility as if each had no higher aim than to cheat the other? If you are a sportsman, you will treat your rival a little better than yourself, then play hard and beat him if you can; and whether you beat him or not, you will do nothing in or before or after the game to forfeit his friendship or your own self-respect. No team-mate, no captain, no coach, can be made responsible for your honor. In questions of fair and foul you are your own captain, your own coach, your own whole team, and need never be defeated.

You belong to a college that takes pride in democracy; and you are bound as inevitably makers of Yale College to guard this democracy with jealous care. Never forget that the only true democracy is not the equalizing of men but the adjustment of opportunity, the recognition of superiority wherever found; not the leveling of all but the enabling of every man to find the level that is his own. This is an important point, which is often overlooked. The Athenian method of choosing magistrates by lot implies either extraordinarily high intelligence in the average man or reckless disregard of common safety. Some persons, while poor, talk as if only the poor were meritorious; yet only a few would remain poor. Some talk as if every member of an old family were a 'highbrow,' whereas a highbrow may or may not be a member of an old family, and a member of an old family may or may not be a highbrow. A highbrow, it has been wisely said, is a person whose education is too much for his intelligence. I have heard a man, and not a small man either, talk as if nobody who wears a fancy waistcoat could be of much use: yet I know the wearer of alarming waistcoats who has won the croix de guerre — and indeed only a man of courage could wear waistcoats like his. Dr. Holmes in 'The Autocrat of the Breakfast Table' reminds us that some of the great soldiers of the world were great dandies also. President Eliot once pointed out that, though Washington's clothes and Lincoln's clothes were quite different in origin and texture, both men were of service to their country. As a college officer who has had unusual opportunities to look into the lives of students, I can testify that eleven years in the Dean's office did much to correct my views of rich and poor at college. In a general way I had accepted the common opinion that nearly all needy students are nobly ambitious to learn and come to college for that purpose, whereas nearly all rich students come to secure or to maintain social standing; and that the majority of the rich students are licentious and lazy. Certainly poor men have an incentive to work which rich men lack, and poor men are often among the finest men in the college; but among the poor men are some of the selfish, crowding, ambitious and mean-spirited and some of the 'cheap sports'; and among the rich are some of the simplest and cleanest and warmest-hearted boys in the world.

The college man should be consciously or — better — unconsciously the leaven of his community. This is especially true of the man from a great university, which, whatever may be said for the small college, gives its students a wider outlook and charges them with a correspondingly heavier responsibility. An original purpose of the college was the training of missionaries, and though the crop of missionaries appears to have dwindled, all true college men are missionaries of a sort, since they enlighten those about them.

This they do, not merely through public association with good causes, but through the quiet force of educated gentlemen leading clean and intelligent lives. It is true that many college men are not such gentlemen and do not lead such lives; but this is because they have not grasped their opportunities as college men. Those who have grasped their opportunities may be the shyest and the humblest of mortals: yet, even so, they teach the best things in life and teach with irresistible power; for along with their shyness and their humility they have made a duty of courage:

'Go boldly, go serenely, go augustly,
What shall withstand thee then?'

You are here to form independent minds, to build each a solid structure of his own; and remember that you never build solidly if you are too sure. When I was a Freshman, all Freshmen were required to read Plato's version of So-

crates's defence — the 'Apology of Socrates,' it is called, though not in the
modern sense an apology, but rather a
defiance. Socrates tells how the oracle
of Apollo had said that he was the
wisest of men. 'The god must speak the
truth,' he said, 'but how can it be? For
I know nothing.' Then he went to one
after another of those who were reputed
wise, and coming again from each of
them, he said to himself: 'I am wiser
than this man; for he, knowing nothing,
believes that he knows much, whereas
I, knowing nothing, know that I know
nothing.' The truth of this story is
profound. Deliver us from the Freshman who 'knows it all.' 'I had rather
not know so much,' said a once famous
American humorist, 'than know so
many things that ain't so.'

Yet every man who truly lives, does
his own thinking, — forms his own
opinions, and, when occasion calls, expresses them without fear. Much that

is worse than nonsense is still taught about 'leading one's own life'; the popular doctrine of leading one's own life is a doctrine of selfishness that yields certain disaster: but in one sense every man should lead his own life. The old poet writing of him

> 'Whose armor is his honest thought,
> And simple truth his utmost skill,'

adds, you remember, —

> 'This man is freed from servile bands
> Of hope to rise, or fear to fall.'

The youth who, as the saying is, 'has his ear to the ground,' or who watches the weathercock on the minds of those to whose club he aspires, is only an imitation of a man and is easily recognizable as such: he may get into the club; but he has no standing there. If we are in this world for anything, we are here to express the best that is in us, which, however commonplace in itself, has, if we express it simply and directly, a touch of something a little different from any other man's expression of it, inasmuch as no two men are exactly alike. If through want of sincerity we throw away that difference, we throw away the one thing that we can contribute by thought and speech to the lives of other men. Without surliness or sourness — even with perfect courtesy — we may be ourselves. In our studies we need not, if I may borrow a figure of speech from President Lowell, be either sponges or syringes, to soak up knowledge or to suck it in and squirt it out; we should, rather, be engines, and what we learn should become a motive power.

So, also, in our habits of life a certain independence is much easier than we are disposed to think it. If we believe not merely in keeping sober but in not drinking at all, it is simple and by no means hard to put our belief in practice. We have to take a little cheap

raillery, and unless we parade our ab-
stinence as a virtue, that is all: nobody
worth counting will think the worse of
us. Other people's approval is pleasant
and encouraging; our own approval is,
for some of us, desperately hard to get:
but something, if not much, of our own
approval, some touch of self-respect, we
must have if we are to live at all; and
there are few more unsuccessful moves
on the chessboard of life than pleasing
or pacifying somebody else by the loss
of respect for ourselves. Managers and
coaches of athletic teams have often
sent downright lies to the press, because
unwilling to tell the truth and equally
unwilling to say nothing for fear that
the reporters may say, out of spite, un-
pleasant and depressing things about
the players: but a coach who will lose
so much to gain so little, and an athlete
who is seriously disturbed by what the
sporting section says of him are pretty
weak brethren, after all.

'Fear not, Cesario,' says Olivia in 'Twelfth Night,'

'Fear not, Cesario; ....
  Be that thou know'st thou art, and then thou art
  As great as that thou fear'st.'

'If thou workest at that which is before thee,' says Marcus Aurelius, 'following right reason seriously, vigorously, calmly, without allowing any thing else to distract thee, but keeping thy divine part pure, as if thou shouldst be bound to give it back immediately; if thou holdest to this, expecting nothing, fearing nothing, but satisfied with thy present activity according to nature, and with heroic truth in every word and sound which thou utterest, thou wilt live happy. And there is no man who is able to prevent this.'

'If I do not keep step with others,' says Thoreau, 'it is because I hear a different drummer. Let a man step to the music which he hears, however measured and however far away.'

Do not forget that a college education, though it tends to conventionalize men outwardly by civilizing them, develops rather than suppresses individuality. It may be true, as a cynical professor remarked, that 'thinking is the last exercise in which students employ their minds'; it is truer that college men, though they think too little, think more than other men, since to them more than to other men is open the world's great treasury of thought and its value made known. Mr. Dooley distinguishes between the 'college of spacheless thought' and 'the college of thoughtless spache.' See to it that you do your part to keep Yale College a college of speaking thought and thinking speech. Failure to do your own thinking is not to face life honestly; failure to speak out at the right time is not to face your neighbors honestly, not

to face honestly those whom you live
with and whom you should live for.

I say 'whom you should live for.' 'To
be less and less personal in one's de-
sires and workings is the great matter,'
says Matthew Arnold. 'My city, so far
as I am Antoninus, is Rome,' says
Marcus Aurelius, 'but so far as I am a
man it is the world.' In those days not
long ago when the literally rotten doctrine of 'leading one's own life' found
such favor, when sceptical of a world
to come, men and women were deter-
mined to get what they could out of this
present world, when to bear one another's burdens and thus to fulfil the
law of Christ was not merely unfashion-
able, as it had always been, but un-
philosophical also in the cancerous philosophy of an overrated nation, the evil
doctrine bore as its fruit a ghastly and
terrific war. Then came the natural
consequence of an arrogant nation's ac-
cepting this reversal of the truth for

which Christ lived and died. Then and
only then the world awoke; and nobody
who is morally awake, nobody who is
not drugged with decaying philosophy,
talks of 'leading his own life.'

'I have a rendezvous with death,'
Alan Seeger wrote from the trenches,

> 'I have a rendezvous with Death
> At some disputed barricade,
> When Spring comes back with rustling shade
> And apple-blossoms fill the air —
> I have a rendezvous with Death
> When Spring brings back blue days and fair.
>
> 'It may be he shall take my hand
> And lead me into his dark land
> And close my eyes and quench my breath —
> It may be I shall pass him still.
> I have a rendezvous with Death
> On some scarred slope of battered hill,
> When Spring comes round again this year
> And the first meadow-flowers appear.
>
> 'God knows 'twere better to be deep
> Pillowed in silk and scented down,
> Where Love throbs out in blissful sleep,
> Pulse nigh to pulse, and breath to breath,
> Where hushed awakenings are dear . . .

But I've a rendezvous with Death
At midnight in some flaming town,
When Spring trips north again this year,
And I to my pledged word am true,
I shall not fail that rendezvous.'

Insignificant people, pleasure-loving people, are now revealed as men. Even in worldly New York, it is said, no young man has standing unless he is in the service. Middle-aged men of business who look as if they had never heard of an ideal, give up profitable commercial enterprises or high-salaried positions for posts of hardship or of death. Men apparently useless put to shame some of us who thought ourselves their betters, by disclosing what has been called 'the fortitude and the moral splendor with which man may confront the indignity of his lot,' by eagerness to risk all for a cause so impersonal as the liberty of the whole world. Fifty years ago Emerson wrote of those who fought in the Civil War

'Though love repine, and reason chafe,
There came a voice without reply; —'

He wrote also

'Who shall nerve heroic boys
To hazard all in Freedom's fight?'

and

'So nigh is grandeur to our dust,
So near is God to man,
When Duty whispers low, *Thou must,*
The youth replies, *I can.*'

Who indeed should nerve these heroic boys, who if not the college? Among the youth who leap to the post of danger are first and foremost, now and always, young college graduates and college students. These are times that try men's faith, but give instant justification to their faith in young men. When we think of the black terror that seems to envelop the world, when we learn that the arts of civilization have been yoked to the instincts of the savage and the assassin and the tyrant for the domination of the earth, there comes to us as a light through the darkness the glowing spirit of American youth. 'Our boys,' we say, 'have done well; and our college boys' have vindicated the college by making clear to the nations that its ideal — and its accomplishment — is not merely the development of a scholar, but, before all, the training of a man.'

THE END